A GRIM ALMANAC OF

SHROPSHIRE

A GRIM ALMANAC OF
SHROPSHIRE

SAMANTHA LYON

The
History
Press

First published 2013
The History Press
The Mill, Brimscombe Port
Stroud, Gloucestershire, GL5 2QG
www.thehistorypress.co.uk

© Samantha Lyon, 2013

The right of Samantha Lyon to be identified as the Author
of this work has been asserted in accordance with the
Copyright, Designs and Patents Act 1988.

British Library Cataloguing in Publication Data.
A catalogue record for this book is available from the British Library.

ISBN 978 0 7524 8646 8

Typesetting and origination by The History Press
Printed in Great Britain

CONTENTS

ACKNOWLEDGEMENTS

Despite the murders, the suicides, the thefts and the accidents, compiling this book has been an incredible experience. I would like to thank my editor, Matilda Richards, for giving me this opportunity and for her patience and assistance. For their constant help, I would like to thank the staff at Shropshire Archives and the contributors to the online Shrewsbury Forum. I would also like to thank my partner Simon Halse for his support and, more importantly, for all the coffee. Finally, I would love to thank my amazing parents, Alex and Judy Lyon, for introducing me to Shropshire and for their constant encouragement.

INTRODUCTION

The events and information collected and revealed in the following pages were compiled from a combination of newspaper archives, websites and books. As I was conducting this research I developed a new and ardent appreciation for the information age, as well as an incredible respect for anyone who had to conduct research before the advent of the internet. Without my aging laptop and my temperamental internet connection, I would have been completely lost.

When I was first given this exciting project, a fair number of people expressed doubts that peaceable old Shropshire possessed enough of a grim history to fill the pages. I disagreed, knowing that I had the freedom to look centuries into the past – but at the time I didn't entirely appreciate the amount of depravity and wickedness that Shropshire has witnessed. Research would soon reveal the hidden history of terrible crimes and unfortunate accidents which transpired in a county that, at first, seems to be so safe and friendly. It is now entirely clear that scenic views and relaxing country lanes can prove a perfect cover in exactly the same way that winning smiles can conceal a naughty child's misdeed.

Considering the unpleasant events that the research trudged up, it is strange how much I enjoyed the entire process. However, there was one thing that caused a certain amount of frustration: discovering a perfectly morbid and macabre event, only to find that there was no specific date that could be attributed to it. As you can imagine, words like 'approximately' or 'circa' were the bane of my existence and of no help at all when your job is to assign to each occurrence a specific date.

Some of the incidents are immeasurably cruel, some less so, and a few are almost amusing (in a sinister sort of way). It has become apparent that far more information exists regarding murders or attempted murders than about any other type of crime. Throughout history, our newspapers have been crammed full with every available gory detail, from the act itself through to the sentencing. The public has always been captivated by murder, and it isn't a preoccupation that has abated over time. Perhaps we will always possess a morbid fascination with human cruelty, as it goes so far against the social norms we live by and the values most of us revere. Many cases presented here defy belief, and in most the motive falls far short of being satisfactory.

Following a guilty verdict, a myriad of punishments were available. For the more serious crimes, such as murder or rape, hanging was the favoured form of retribution. The justification behind capital punishment stretches far back into history and is based somewhat on the biblical concept of 'an eye for an eye'. It was thought – and is still thought, by some – that such a sentence would act as a deterrent, preventing similar future offences, though this argument often provokes heated debate. Hangings were also frequently doled out for crimes we would now consider extremely minor, such as the theft of a cow or sheep. Once upon a time people regularly risked their lives for a sheep or two, perhaps proving that a public hanging wasn't a sufficient deterrent after all. Salopian locals loved a public hanging. Whether you resented the accused or secretly sympathised with them and hoped for a reprieve, hangings would often attract thousands of spectators. In fact, some loved a good execution so much that they would ask for the day off work so they could take in a hanging and then go on to do something else afterwards too, to make a real day of it. Unfortunately for those who thrived on the drama, the law evolved and public hangings came to an end. The first private hanging in Shrewsbury occurred after William Samuels was convicted of murder. He was hanged on the 28 July 1886, using the timbers from the old scaffold. The execution was conducted by a Yorkshireman by the name of James Berry, who was picked from over 2,000 other applicants. Berry was eventually to execute 117 people over his career, at £10 per execution (in addition to travel expenses) – a modern equivalent of over £1,000.

In addition to hanging, punishment was seen in the forms of stocks, gibbets, imprisonment with hard labour, whipping and transportation. For those accused of witchcraft, burning at the stake was an old favourite, something which proved unfortunate for Mrs Foxall, who was executed in this manner in the Dingle in 1647.

Researching and writing about 365 events has produced quite a mixed bag. Some of the incidents left me appreciating the best in our human nature: for example, when Edward Neville Richards risked his life to save a pony, or when Kenneth Raymond Cooper saved the lives of his workmates – at the cost of his own life – on a demolition site. Other incidents left me completely despairing of it. There were altogether too many incidents of children dying at the hands of their own parents, an act most of us can't even imagine. For those of you with an interest in crime and misfortune, I hope you enjoy the following stories and all their grisly details.

Samantha Lyon, 2013

JANUARY

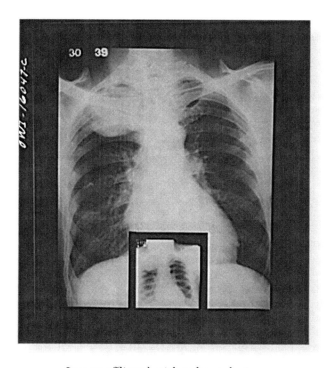

Lungs afflicted with tuberculosis.
(Library of Congress, LC-USW3-016047-C)

1 **JANUARY 1939** In the past tuberculosis claimed a great number of lives and destroyed many households. The best chance for a complete recovery involved a stay in an isolation hospital, as general hospitals had a tendency to turn away patients with the notoriously contagious disease. In the early twentieth century the situation was dire in Shropshire, and pulmonary tuberculosis killed over 120 people per year. This meant that it took more lives than all other infectious diseases combined. By 1907 the only institution in Shropshire that would accept patients was the Shirlett Sanatorium, and by 1918 Shirlett was running at full capacity. Until 1931, Shropshire County Council was paying 83 per cent of each patient's maintenance costs. Unfortunately, however, even this proved insufficient, and the sanatorium ran up a huge debt. Shirlett was forced to ask the council to increase their contributions by a further 9 per cent. By 1938 the situation hadn't improved, and there were worries that patients would have to be sent away. Thankfully for the patients, however, from the 1 January 1939 the council agreed to pay the extra money, and the sanatorium was able to stay open.

2 **JANUARY 1849** On this day, in Acton Burnell, PC John Micklewright came out the worse for the wear after a fight with local labourer Charles Colley. After a good few drinks in the Stags Head, an inebriated Colley was ready for combat. PC Micklewright was called to deal with this difficult customer. He escorted Colley from the pub and told him to go home. Colley flatly refused, and eventually grew so angry that he actually attacked Micklewright, beating him and breaking his leg. Micklewright was looked after by a local doctor, and was admitted to the Royal Salop Infirmary soon afterwards. Sadly, however, the injured policeman died of his wounds fifteen days later. During court proceedings Colley tried to prove that he did not intend to kill Micklewright, and that he had no idea the man was a policeman. He claimed that his actions were carried out in self defence, and that he therefore lacked the malicious intent necessary for a charge of murder. After only two minutes of deliberation, the jury returned a verdict of manslaughter. The judge believed that the jury had been extremely

lenient but accordingly Colley was given ten years' transportation. To make matters worse, this assault occurred at a time before social security or pensions, and there was no one to provide Micklewright's grieving widow with financial support. She was forced into a workhouse, where she died soon after.

3   JANUARY **1810** On 2 January a fire was sparked in the Meadow Pit in Madeley. At the time the fire caught hold, thirteen men were working underground. Rather luckily, all the men working in the pit managed to escape to the surface, from a depth of 1,000ft, without a scratch. However, a tragedy occurred on this, the following day, when four men descended into the pit to determine the extent of the damage the fire had caused: all four were suffocated by the sulphur fumes.

4   JANUARY **1951** Frank Griffin was executed on this day for the murder of landlady Jane Edge. The crime took place on the 6 September 1950 at the Queen's Head Pub, Ketley, where Griffin, intent on robbery, beat Edge to death. He fled the scene with coins and notes crammed in his pockets. The last thing the victim said was that the money he stole 'would do him no good'. At his trial, Griffin insisted that he had not intended to kill Edge and was unaware that the damage he inflicted would end her life. He insisted that Edge would have survived his vicious assault had she not been 'over-nourished' with an 'enlarged heart'. Judge Cassels swiftly dismissed this excuse: when you commit a violent act, he informed the prisoner, you have to take your victims as you find them. As a capital sentence was handed down, Griffin could only have been thinking about the landlady's last words, and how right she had been.

5   JANUARY **1937** From *The Times*: 'On the arrival of a Belgian airliner here from Cologne this afternoon it was reported that one of the ten passengers, whose name is given as Mr Max Wenner of Bathcote Hall, Leebotwood, Shropshire, had fallen out of the machine during the flight at an altitude of about 3,000ft. The aeroplane [...] was passing through

clouds at the time of the accident. Mr Wenner was in the lavatory of the aeroplane at the time. The pilot stated that he felt a slight shock. It is stated that the outside canvas of the aeroplane was found to be torn. The body of Mr Wenner was found, according to news received at Croydon, in the Meuse district of Belgium last night.'

6   JANUARY 1887   On this day the local newspapers reported on the events of the previous day's Shropshire Quarter Sessions. It came to light that Henry Clarence Williams, a physician and surgeon, along with his wife, Mary, had been charged with assaulting their daughter. The assault occurred on the 28 October 1886 when the girl, Gladys, was the subject of an unflattering report by her governess, who informed Henry and Mary that their daughter had not been paying attention. Her parents initially punished the child with a diet of dry bread, but soon decided that this was not enough of a penance. They took her to the nursery and shut the door to secure their privacy. In court, the servants said that they had heard the child scream for half an hour before Williams emerged, fetched a decanter of port, and returned to the room – where the screams began anew. One servant said that they saw the doctor standing near his child with a whip in his hand. The same servant, who was deeply distressed by the girl's treatment, actually passed out when she saw the extent of the bruises on the girl's lower body. The incident was reported to the police, and the local doctor testified that considerable violence had been inflicted with a riding whip. The defendants were ultimately found guilty of common assault and were forced to pay a fine and court costs.

7   JANUARY 1932   Due to a severe overflowing of the River Severn, two chimneys collapsed through the roof of the 'Poor Law Institution' at Bridgnorth. The chimneys fell straight through the sitting room and larder, causing a considerable amount of damage. The master of the house, along with the matron of the institution and a baby, were having dinner at the time that the debris fell, but thankfully no one was injured.

8   JANUARY 1924 On this day, the media reported on the death of a local celebrity, Mr William Shakespeare Childe-Pemberton (66), who died on the 5 January at Kinlet Hall after a short illness. He was a well-known writer of memoirs, as well as being extremely knowledgeable on art and history. Two notable works of Childe-Pemberton's are *The Romance of Princess Amelia* and *Elizabeth Blount and Henry the Eighth, with Some Account of her Surroundings*. The building of Kinlet Hall was accomplished by demolishing the surrounding villages, forcing the villagers to move. The space surrounding the building was then turned into parkland.

9   JANUARY 1839 At the Shropshire Quarter Sessions, Mr E. Edmonds, who was a coroner in Oswestry, was indicated for violating the Registration of Births and Deaths Act. It seems that during his time as coroner Edmonds failed to send to the district registrars the death certificates for his death inquests; when the certificates were demanded of him, he refused to hand them over. The jury returned a guilty verdict, and the honourable chairman summed up by reminding the court that Acts of Parliament must be obeyed, even if an individual disagreed with them, for the preservation of order.

10   JANUARY 1816 On this day Martha Riley, a single mother with a young child, was found guilty of stealing a few potatoes from a neighbouring garden. Riley, who was not married, had no other means of support. However, the owner of the potatoes had little sympathy and called for the constable. He soon took her to Shrewsbury for her trial, and she was sentenced to one year's hard labour. The child served the time with her in Shrewsbury Gaol.

Single mother Martha Riley and her young child both served time in Shrewsbury Gaol, Howard Street. (Photo by Samantha Lyon)

11 JANUARY 1832 The local papers reported that three men – Isaac Skit (alias Isaac Powys), Emmanuel Shepherd and John Corfield, all of whom were colliers – had been indicted for 'riotously assembling' on 8 December 1831. After meeting, the small group then proceeded to Steeraway Lime Works, where they recruited further rioters. The jury, however, decided to dismiss the charges. When the chairman discharged the prisoners he said that he hoped they would go home 'feeling lucky', and would appreciate the 'forgiving nature' of the jury. He reminded them that the law was put in place to protect them, and he hoped that, as such, they would abide by it in the future.

12 JANUARY 1867 At this time there were extremely heavy floods in Shropshire. The Severn had recently iced over and subsequently thawed, causing the river to flood to an extent unseen since 1852. The fields surrounding the river were submerged for hundreds of acres, and at one point hedges disappeared completely under the water. In Smithfield Road, where a row of houses were enclosed by water, households were forced to live upstairs and to use boats in order to get around town.

13 JANUARY 1790 An inn in Ellesmere was the subject of an article in *The Times* on this day. The paper reported that the following poem had been scrawled on a window:

> Dust is lighter than a feather,
> The wind much lighter is than either;
> But, Alas! frail woman kind
> Is far much lighter than the wind.

Beneath this, in different handwriting, was a riposte:

> Friend, you mistake the matter quite!
> How can you say that a woman's light?
> Poor Cornuo swears, throughout his life,
> His heaviest plague has been a wife!

14 JANUARY 1866 Before the birth of serology (the science of analysing blood), murder trials were often reliant on the informed opinions of doctors or police officers. These men would be asked to decide if blood found at a crime scene (or on a suspect) came from a human or from an animal. The case of Edward Edwards (18) was one of these cases. Edwards was murdered at Duddlewich Mill on this day. He left before breakfast to feed the pigs. Eventually, when he did not return, a search was instituted, and Edwards was found, bleeding, bruised and very near death, in a lower room in his uncle's mill. His skull was fractured, and several inches of bone were protruding into his brain. His hands were also cut – injuries sustained whilst defending himself against his attacker, it was presumed. When Edwards died, charges were brought against his uncle, John Meredith, on the basis that a pair of his (Meredith's) trousers had been discovered which were covered with blood. This item of clothing was sent to Professor Alfred Swaine Taylor at Guy's Hospital for examination. However, luckily for the uncle, Swaine Taylor explained at the inquest that it was not possible for him to distinguish whether it was animal blood and human. Meredith was therefore acquitted.

Prof. Swaine Taylor of Guy's Hospital claimed there was no way to distinguish human blood from animal blood, which resulted in Meredith's acquittal. (THP)

15 JANUARY 1785 On this day Robert Cole was found guilty of begging around Wellington Parish. His punishment was to be publically whipped all the way from Shrewsbury Market Hall to the gaol, where he served a six-month sentence – only to be publically whipped once again upon his release. Public displays of whipping officially came to an end in Shrewsbury in 1840.

16 JANUARY 1668 On this day Francis Talbot, the 11th Earl of Shrewsbury and 11th Earl of Waterford, duelled with George Villiers, 2nd Duke of Buckingham, who was the lover of Talbot's wife, Lady Anna Maria Brudenell. Samuel Pepys wrote of:

> the duell yesterday between the Duke of Buckingham ... and my Lord of Shrewsbury ... and all about my Lady Shrewsbury, who is a whore, and is at this time, and hath for a great while been, a whore to the Duke of Buckingham. And so her husband challenged him, and they met yesterday in a close near Barne-Elmes, and there fought: and my Lord Shrewsbury is run through the body, from the right breast through the shoulder: and Sir John Talbot all along up one of his armes ... This will make the world think that the king hath good councillors about him, when the Duke of Buckingham, the greatest man about him, is a fellow of no more sobriety than to fight about a whore ... I shall not be much sorry [if Buckingham should get into trouble for the fight] that we may have some sober man ... to assist in the Government.

These injuries ultimately resulted in Talbot's early death. His wife was rumoured to have dressed up as a page and held Villiers' horse in order to view the duel. She later moved into Buckingham's house, which was also home to his wife, causing an enormous scandal.

17 JANUARY 1887 When part of the roof of the Shrewsbury railway station collapsed under the weight of the snow piled on top of it, William Heath, a local town councillor and coal merchant, was killed on

Shrewsbury railway station is said to be haunted by the ghost of Councillor William Heath. (Photo by Samantha Lyon)

platform three. An inquest held on this day ruled the unfortunate event an accidental death. Sightings of his ghost have been reported on platform three since Heath's demise. Come nightfall, it is said, he can be seen waiting around on the platform for his train.

18 JANUARY 1911 An employee of the Ketley Grant Colliery by the name of Edward Morgan (24) was killed on this day, along with two other men. The three workers were 'holing' when a large 5-yard length of coal fell over and buried them alive. The sad incident may have been avoided had 'under-sprags' (a device, usually a post or bar, used to support mining roofs) been used.

19 JANUARY 1810 An inquest was held into the death of Elizabeth Williams (15), who had been a servant to Mrs Ridley of St Alkmund's Square. On the Monday prior to this inquest, Williams, feeling unwell, retired to bed. She ate only a little broth for the rest of the day, but her condition quickly deteriorated. By the evening she was dead. As she had been downstairs when she perished, her replacement was forced to carry her corpse upstairs. Elizabeth's body was placed on the bed, where she remained until the 18th.

When she was asked to explain why she had left the body there, Mrs Ridley replied that she had wanted to leave the girl, just as she was when she died, until such a time as her father could see her. At the inquiry Mrs Ridley was also asked why she had not informed the girl's sister, who lived nearby, of her death. Mrs Ridley claimed that she had 'forgotten where she lived'. The sister rejected this story: she told the inquest that she had come to visit, but had been told that Elizabeth was 'not in' and further, that she was not allowed to wait at the house for her return. A neighbour attested that she had heard violent groans coming from the house for several hours on the evening the servant died. An acquaintance of the deceased also claimed that Williams had often complained of being deprived of food and mistreated by her employers. Despite all the above evidence, the jury at the inquest decided that there was not sufficient information to show that Elizabeth had been murdered, although they had reason to suspect the deceased had been improperly treated.

Elizabeth Williams lived with her employer, Mrs Ridley, in St Alkmund's Square. (Photo by Samantha Lyon)

20 JANUARY 1900 When lighting a lamp on a ferry in Jackfield, near Ironbridge, John Harrison (72) fell backwards into the Severn and was swept away by the aggressive waters, as witnessed by fellow boatman Henry Wild and school teacher Jane Ellen Blocksidge. Forty-one days later he was found, dead and his body in the late stages of decomposition, on the shore of the River Severn at Bridgnorth.

21 JANUARY **1949** *The Times* today reported the death of local farmer James A. Davies of Lower Eyton Farm, Alberbury. He passed on at the Royal Salop Infirmary on the 19 January after a horrible accident: he was gored by a bull on his farm. The incident occurred when Davies was out on his farm feeding his calves: the bull, which had been tethered, managed to break its chain and instantly attacked Davies.

22 JANUARY **1816** On this date, local businessman and registrar-general of Shropshire Thomas Eyton died at his home in Wellington. It was widely believed that the death occurred following a short illness, but in fact it was later established that Eyton had committed suicide following the failure of his business, which had fallen into substantial tax arrears.

23 JANUARY **1936** Drusilla Pilliner (55) died in hospital after being involved in a road accident at Wrottesley. She was one of four people, including Jesse Broome, William Talbot Pilliner and Cecil Franklin, who were injured in the accident when their car collided with a coal lorry on the main road between Wolverhampton and Shrewsbury.

24 JANUARY **1928** At this time, the Ministry of Health issued a circular to the Boards of Guardians regarding outbreaks of smallpox around the country. In the twentieth century an estimated 300 million people died from the disease. However, the numbers had been even higher before Edward Jenner developed a vaccine in 1796, based on his observation that people who contracted cowpox did not go on to contract smallpox. In this year the Ministry of Health revealed that a case of smallpox had been discovered in Wollerton, a small village in North Shropshire. The World Health Organisation did not officially announce the eradication of the disease until 1979. Nonetheless, it remains one of only two infectious diseases which have officially been eradicated.

25 JANUARY 1826 In this year an incident in Market Drayton caught national media attention after magistrates discovered that a mentally handicapped man had been locked up by his family in squalid conditions for several years. Some years before, it was revealed, William Smith and his sister had detained their brother, George, in the attic and boarded up the windows. The Smiths claimed that keeping their brother in this impromptu prison was necessary, as light 'threw him into fits'. They also added that if the windows were not covered with boards he would punch through the glass. However, it is more likely that this action was taken in order to hide George from the sight of others. In fact, the duo perpetuated a myth that the house was haunted in order to deter visitors with prying eyes. In 1826 a servant quit her position with the Smiths and went to work for a neighbouring magistrate. She promptly told him about George and, on 25 January, Revd Henry Delves Broughton and Mr Eld went to the house and demanded to see the prisoner. The sight inside was truly shocking: the attic was filthy, and covered with excrement and straw. They swiftly removed George Smith from the house and placed him in the county asylum in Stafford. He died there three years later and was returned, at the request of the family, so that he could be buried in Bucklestone. The story gets stranger still: in 1883, a workman accidentally hit the coffin with a pick. The box was found to be empty.

26 JANUARY 1862 On the 3 February 1862, Jack and Peter Tolley were brought before a jury at Shrewsbury and charged with the murder of John Preece. Preece was a labourer on the Shrewsbury and Hereford line. On the 26 January he went out with workmates to the Bridge Inn in Dorrington, where they met the Tolley brothers. They stayed at the inn until 9 p.m., whereupon they all departed. Preece and the Tolley brothers had not been walking long before a dispute erupted. The fight allegedly involved the accusation that Preece could not do as much work, or work as hard, as the other men on the team. During the fight that followed Jack Tolley stabbed the victim. When Dr Glover reached the site he found Preece lying on his side in the road, sporting a wound 3in long in his right side, a puncture that passed through the abdominal muscle. Unfortunately, the wound proved fatal, and Preece died on 29 January. The jury found Jack guilty of murder, but as there was not sufficient evidence to convict Peter he was discharged.

27 JANUARY 1902 On this day a coroner by the name of Mr F.H. Potts conducted an inquiry into the bodies of single mother Harriett Meyrick Edwards (22) and her daughter Charlsey Margaret Edwards (4). Both bodies had suffered severe burns. Harriet sported marks on her face and neck, and her lips and tongue were also badly blistered. The child was even more drastically burned, and both the mother and daughter had their hands clenched, suggesting that their deaths had been painful. It was concluded that the deaths were caused by carbolic-acid poisoning, and that Harriett had wilfully murdered her young child and then killed herself during a bout of insanity. After Charlsey was born, Harriett had remained very much in love with Harry Adams, the child's father. However, when it became clear that Adams did not share her devotion, Harriett became unhinged. Evidence was brought to light to suggest that Harriett's mental health had been worsening for some time. She had recently approached a local chemist in Broseley, one George Egglestone, to apply for some laudanum – she was having difficulty sleeping, she said. He informed her that he was unable to supply her since it was a prescription drug, and she left his shop. The inquest could not discover the source of the acid with which Harriett had taken her own life. On 2 February the *Wellington Journal* revealed the contents of her suicide letter, which stated that Harriett was 'tired of life' and that she was 'sorry to cause so much bother'. She seemed to be under the misapprehension that Adams was going to commit suicide along with her: 'she [Charlsey] will have no one to look after her when we have gone,' she wrote. 'Me and Harry have resolved to die together. Nothing to live for here. I can't write any more. Tell poor old dad not to worry.'

28 JANUARY 1890 Today the Severn overflowed to a near record-breaking level and thousands of acres were submerged. The town was submerged in several feet of water, and the streets of Shrewsbury resembled

The River Severn, which overflowed and forced people from their homes in 1890. (Photo by Samantha Lyon)

a canal. In order to get from one location to another, boats and temporary bridges had to be used. People were forced from the lower rooms of their homes, and some had to be removed from their homes entirely.

29 JANUARY 1952 On this day Plaish Hall in Cardington was listed as a Grade I building. The building has an incredibly interesting yet slightly morbid history. It was built for Judge William Leighton in the sixteenth century. However, one thing remained to finish the job: the judge needed a chimney stack for his new roof. When a builder named Sherrett came to his courtroom, the judge proposed a deal: he would spare Sherrett the capital punishment his offence otherwise warranted if Sherrett agreed to build the chimney stack. The builder readily agreed and completed the job – but as soon as the stack was finished the judge went back on his word and had the man hanged. Ghost stories about the house are widespread: according to one legend, the chimney sometimes drips blood ...

30 JANUARY 1931 Albert Edward Deverell (43) and his wife Gwendoline were found dead in their home at Carding Mill. Albert, who had been a cashier at Lloyds bank in Church Stretton, was found on the floor of his bedroom with a pistol in his hand; Gwendoline was found lying in the bed with a bullet in her head. The grisly scene was discovered by Police Sergeant Barklay; he had received a telephone call from Deverell's distraught manager, who had found a suicide note written by his client. The letter indicated that Deverell had been suffering financially. He could not see a way out, and decided that he was 'going over the line' – and that he was taking his wife along for the ride.

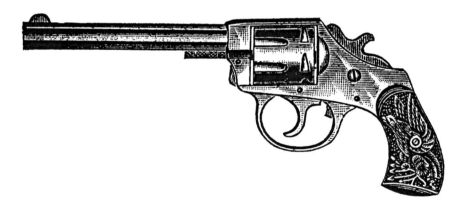

31 JANUARY 1679 Reverend Robert Foulkes was executed on this day for the murder of his newborn baby. Before the news of the crime became public, Foulkes had been the popular vicar of St Peter's in Stanton Lacy. A few years before the crime Foulkes had taken in a young orphaned lady, with whom he began a relationship – despite the fact that he already had a wife and two children. Perhaps unavoidably, the girl became pregnant. First Foulkes attempted to abort the baby. When this was unsuccessful, he moved his pregnant mistress to an isolated location, far from prying eyes and his jealous wife, where she could come to term and deliver the baby. In York Buildings, in the Strand, the girl gave birth, though she was denied the normal medical attention that most mothers receive. Instead, Foulkes alone helped deliver the baby – and then he quietly murdered him by thrusting his body into the 'house of office', or the privy. They then returned to Stanton Lacy and tried to resume a normal life. All might have gone well had not an observant parishioner realised that the girl, to all appearances, had recently given birth. Upon questioning the girl broke down and confessed everything, and the authorities became involved. Both the young lady and Foulkes were charged with the murder and entered pleas of 'not guilty'. The gentlewoman was found not guilty, and was generally regarded with much sympathy. Foulkes, however, was found guilty and sentenced to death.

FEBRUARY

King George V was challenged by Anthony Hall,
a former member of the Shropshire Police, who
believed that he was the rightful heir to the throne.
(LC-DIG-ggbain-04906 Library of Congress,
George Grantham Bain Collection)

1   **FEBRUARY 1883**   This was the last day that Mary Elizabeth Mayo (12) was seen alive. Her father, Thomas Mayo, and her step-mother were regularly abusive toward Mary Elizabeth and her four siblings. Cries of pain were often heard from their house, and they were usually to be seen with injuries or bruises. On 2 February, while searching for duck eggs, Joseph Bates found the head of a young girl in the shallow water. After considerable confusion and investigation, the head was revealed to have belonged to Mary Elizabeth. During the trial, the prosecution suggested that Mary Elizabeth's death had been the result of repetitive blows to the head. After her death the wicked parents dismembered her and bundled up the body parts, discarding some and burning the rest. Mrs Mayo was found guilty of manslaughter and received a sentence of twenty years' penal servitude. If the court had not believed her story – that she had not intended to kill the young girl, but only to beat her and to enforce discipline – she would have been sentenced to death. Mr Mayo received eighteen months of hard labour for dismembering the body. The public generally agreed that the duo had got off lightly.

2   **FEBRUARY 1931**   Anthony Hall had been part of the Shropshire Police for eight years before leaving, in 1927, to go to Canada. Hall insisted he was far more than a simple police officer, however, and stirred up a huge amount of trouble when he proclaimed himself to be the rightful heir to the throne. He was convinced that he was the descendant of an illegitimate child of Anne Boleyn and Henry VIII. After Queen Elizabeth died in 1603, he said, his family should have inherited the Crown, making him the twenty-third descendant of the Tudors. Hall told his public that King George V should immediately be beheaded, and Hall crowned King Anthony I in his stead. On 2 February 1931 Hall wrote to the king directly, saying that 'the whole world has been hoodwinked for 328 years' and informing him that he was officially claiming the Crown. According to documents held at the Kew National Archive, the king wanted Hall sectioned. The claimant was eventually fined £25 for disturbing the peace, and disappeared soon afterwards.

3 FEBRUARY 1582 John Prestige, alias Hill, killed his wife by throwing her off a bridge and into the Severn, causing her to drown. Following a trial, Prestige was executed and placed in a gibbet by the side of the Abbey Mill, near the English Bridge. This location was directly opposite his home. His corpse remained hanging there for three days after his execution to act as a warning to prospective criminals.

River Severn. (Photo by Samantha Lyon)

4 FEBRUARY 1739 Robert Cadman (28), sometimes recorded as Kidman, was a nineteenth-century stuntman. During his time he performed varied and incredible stunts, such as sliding across the River Severn to Gay Meadow on a rope, performing tricks on the way. His sad demise occurred on 2 February, when the rope he was attempting to ride – which ran from the spire of St Mary's Church to the ground – snapped, pitching him to his death. He was buried in St Mary's on this day, and just outside the church remains a commemorative plaque that reads:

Let this small Monument record the name

Of Cadman, and to future time proclaim

How by'n attempt to fly from this high spire

Across the Sabrine he did acquire

His fatal end.

'Twas not for want of skill

Or courage to perform the task he fell,

No, no, a faulty Cord being drawn too tight

Harries his

Soul on high to take her flight

Which bid the Body here beneath good Night.

February 2nd 1739, aged 28.

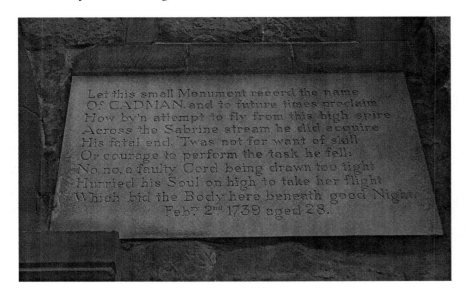

A commemorative plaque for Robert Cadman, located outside St Mary's Church, Dogpole, Shrewsbury. Cadman fell to his death during his final stunt. (Photo by Samantha Lyon)

5 FEBRUARY 1878 George Strange, Thomas Williams and George Allison were indicted for the highway robbery of Thomas Thomas, which occurred on this day near Ellesmere. An argument began shortly after the four men entered

a local pub. Thomas implied, non-too subtly, that Strange had been poaching on his private land. In order to prevent a brawl, the landlord intervened. He warned them not to fight on the premises. The three men left soon after, followed shortly by Thomas Thomas. At a point in the road where Thomas was meant to turn toward his house, the three men came up behind him. Strange knocked the man down; then Williams joined the fight, kicking Thomas in the face and breaking his nose. Thomas claimed that robbery was always the motive for the attack: when he was in the pub, he told the court, the men had been able to see where he kept his money and so, after he was rendered immobile on the floor, they were able to steal his purse. Allison was found not guilty and swiftly acquitted. The other two were found not guilty of highway robbery, but guilty of assault occasioning actual bodily harm. Strange was sentenced to a year in prison with hard labour, and Williams to nine months.

6 **FEBRUARY 1945** A Lancaster bomber, piloted by Flight Sergeant Robert Erskine Plante (31) of Australia, disappeared over Shropshire on this date. Plante had been flying with six other men and had set off from Lindholme Airfield. The mystery remains unsolved, as no wreckage has ever been found. Nothing has been heard of the men since that fateful day. Donald Stokes of Ellesmere, who at the time was the son of the mayor, is believed to have been the last person to hear the aircraft:

A Lancaster bomber, carrying seven men, disappeared over Shropshire in 1945. (Per from Thunder Bay, Canada, Wikimedia Commons)

I remember it because it was my birthday, February 6. In the middle of the night there was a tremendous engine noise. It woke me up and I went to the window. Then, after one-and-a-half minutes, the noise stopped. It did not fade away or die out. It stopped immediately and totally. I had never heard an aircraft making that noise before. It was either engines at extreme power or something [had gone] wrong.

7 FEBRUARY 1938 The local media reported a fire that broke out on the farm of George Burroughs, a resident of Aston, Shifnal. The outhouses, which contained wheat and crops, were set alight and masses of expensive farming equipment were destroyed. On top of this Burroughs lost a good portion of his flock: forty-three of his sheep burned to death.

8 FEBRUARY 1946 Once again the inevitable flooding of the Severn caused chaos in the area, with many main roads, including the ones between Shrewsbury and Welshpool, Welshpool and Oswestry, and Newton and Welshpool, becoming impassable. Cars were abandoned on the watery roads.

9 FEBRUARY 1961 George Riley (21) was hanged on this day for the murder of local widow Adeline Mary Smith (62) on 7 October. Riley was the last man ever to be hanged at the Dana Prison. Adeline Mary lived across the road from Riley. The case was extremely controversial: many people at the time maintained his innocence, and indeed some continue to do so today. His family attempted to secure a reprieve, but were ultimately unsuccessful. The day Riley was executed, the prisoners of the Dana Prison put on what the *Shropshire Star* described as a 'horrifying demonstration'. They created a cacophony by shouting, banging on the rails and whistling, all the while keeping up a refrain of, 'Don't hang George, let Riley go free.'

10 FEBRUARY 1849 Richard Wilson was indicted for the wilful murder of Anne Wilson, his wife, on 10 February. Wilson was a pensioner living in Hankolow, Cheshire, who regularly visited Market Drayton to collect his pension. Traditionally he and his wife would remain until late in the day. On the day in question, the couple had been seen walking by the side of the Shropshire Union Canal, apparently in good humour. It seems that this good mood shifted shortly afterwards, however, when she, becoming wobbly in her drunken state, found she could no longer walk as fast as he demanded. Frustrated, Wilson threatened to throw her into the canal. His wife dismissed this threat, adamant that he would not dare. He then knocked her down. After some harsh words, he helped her back up and they continued on with their walk. All the events mentioned so far were recalled in court by a witness, who also claimed to have heard screams and a cry of 'murder' approximately ten minutes after the couple wandered from sight. The witness next saw Wilson an hour later at Aderly Lock House, and noted the woman's absence. Wilson claimed to have left her near Simon's Bridge, near the canal, where she was waiting for a boat. Her body was discovered in the canal near Betton Wood Bridge at 9 a.m. the next day.

11   FEBRUARY 1894   This day saw a large portion of St Mary's Church spire, the highest point in Shrewsbury town, being blown down, which caused significant damage to the building. *Bloody British History: Shrewsbury* shares more about this event:

> The night of 11 February 1894 saw tremendous gales covering much of the country. In Shrewsbury the wind was already such that, by midday, the *Shrewsbury Chronicle* recorded that, 'its fury [created] general terror and alarm. It was almost impossible to walk along the streets so exceedingly rough was the wind; it was very dangerous too, for bricks, tiles and slates were being dashed from the housetops in all directions.' That evening the storm got worse, and at 9.30 p.m. there was a sudden crash "resembling the discharge of a cannon" and the top 40ft of the spire fell through.

The story goes that the vicar preached that it had been 'thrown down by God' as a result of the town's support for the new (and controversial) theories of Mr Charles Darwin – money to erect a statue of the town's most famous son was being collected at the time. The church, now disused, attracts a great number of visitors each year due to its rich history and its varied collection of stained glass.

12 FEBRUARY 1795 The flood that occurred on this day might be the greatest flood the Severn has ever experienced. The changeable weather was to blame, as the once icy river melted and rose to a height of over 20ft. The supporting pier of the original bridge at Coalport, which was made with timber fifteen years before, was washed away and the susceptible area of Frankwell was drowned in 2m of water.

13 FEBRUARY 1935 Shropshire has an extensive mining history, and it is because of this history that many of the county's villages were able to thrive. However, the occupation regularly proved to be extremely hazardous, with accidents often occurring due to a number of causes. Death could result from rock slides, fires, noxious gases, or falls. Due to the probability of an accident or fatality, miners paid a few pence per week to the Midlands Miners' Fatal Accident Fund, which would serve as a security for the bereaving family. On this day a miner by the name of William Edwards was buried under a fall of rocks in a mine at Habberley. His body was not recovered until the next day.

Miners had hazardous lives and were often victims of rock slides, fires, noxious gases or falls. (Library of Congress)

14 FEBRUARY 1935 Ellen Woof (34) of Market Drayton was charged with bigamy with local labourer William Jefferies (52), and with aiding and abetting the same crime. Far from being angry, Ellen's husband was fully supportive: he said that he wanted his wife to be happy, and this meant allowing her a certain amount of freedom. Shocking as this may seem today, it would have been infinitely more scandalous at the time. Justice Hawke of the Shrewsbury Assizes, on the marriage, remarked that they were a couple with very odd views and that the man and wife were, 'Not very strong on the subject of matrimony except in their desire to get married when they felt inclined.'

15 FEBRUARY 1730 The renowned Revd Dr Thomas Bray died on this day. He was born in Marton, Chirbury, and educated at Oswestry School before attending Oxford University and becoming a celebrated clergyman. During this time he lived in Maryland, USA, as an Anglican representative. Whilst at Maryland he became fascinated with colonial missions and took a great interest in the Native Americans. His efforts helped found what was then known as the Society for the Propagation of the Gospel in Foreign Parts. The Society has a violent side to its history: a long and infamous association with the slave trade. At their Codrington plantation, all slaves were burnt on the chest with a red-hot iron in the shape of an s (for 'Society'). Other cruel devices used at the plantation included the lash, the iron collar and the straightjacket. Ten years after the doctor's death, a shockingly high death rate was recorded there: an estimated 40 per cent of the plantation's slaves perished within three years of arriving.

The seal of the Society for the Propagation of the Gospel in Foreign Parts. (THP)

16 **FEBRUARY 1844** On this day Joseph Willets feloniously set fire to a barn belonging to Joseph Merris of Redhill Farm, Halesowen. Willets was found guilty on 18 March and Mr Baron Parke, when passing the sentence, pointed out that only a few years ago his crime would have been punishable by death. The judge told the prisoner that he felt so strongly about the offence that he almost regretted that the death penalty had been remitted for this crime. Parke went on to give Willets the harshest sentence he could – lifelong transportation.

17 **FEBRUARY 1866** Today the Commissioners for British Asylums reported on the removal of several patients originally from Shropshire from the Lancaster County Asylum. They were perhaps the lucky ones: in the last six months, fifty-nine patients had left the same asylum in a coffin, 'the principal causes being general palsy and epilepsy, phthisis, diseases of the brain, exhaustion after mania, and senile decay; but in two cases inquests had to be held, one man having died suddenly from disease of the heart, and the other having strangled himself.'

18 **FEBRUARY 1945** The 1st Battalion of the King's Shropshire Light Infantry, a regiment of the British Army that was formed in 1881, was ordered to the Middle East and was stationed in Palestine due to the British-Zionist conflict. The 1st Battalion was the regiment which suffered the very first casualty of the Second World War:

A memorial for the First Battalion of the King's Shropshire Light Infantry, who were ordered to the Middle East in 1945. (Photo by Samantha Lyon)

on 9 December 1939, Corporal Thomas Priday of the 1st Battalion was killed by a landmine near Metz.

19 FEBRUARY 1955 A 'wooden horse' that had been gathering dust in the basement of the Shrewsbury Employment Exchange for more than two years was sent on its way to the Imperial War Museum. The horse, built in the RAF station at Shawbury, was a replica of the one used during wartime escapes from StalagLuft 111 in Germany. This modern 'Trojan Horse' was designed to conceal men and tools. Historically, the structure was carted out to a place near the perimeter of the fence. While prisoners exercised above as a means of disguise, other men worked on digging the tunnel below. As the day drew to a close the entrance to the tunnel would be covered with a wooden board and scattered with dirt. The original structure allowed Michael Codner, Eric Williams and Oliver Philpot to make their escape over the course of three months by digging over 100ft using just their feeding bowls.

20 FEBRUARY 1874 This day saw the advent of a horrible railway accident at Church Stretton on the Shrewsbury and Hereford railway. Two platelayers had stepped off one line and onto the other to move out of the way of an approaching train. Simultaneously, and rather unfortunately, another engine came up, unobserved, on the other line and knocked them both down, killing them instantly. The subsequent inquest ruled these 'accidental deaths'.

21 FEBRUARY 1752 Right Revd Samuel Peploe (84), Bishop of Chester, who was the son of a Little Dawley farmer and who was baptised at Dawley Parva, died on this day. During his life he built up a reputation for being very outspoken about his dissatisfaction with the Roman Catholic Church. When he was in charge of the church at Preston, for example, he preached a sermon in support of King George I. He also defied the Jacobites who were then holding the city by loudly reading the prayers for the king. When a soldier approached him with a drawn sword and demanded that he pray instead for the Old Pretender, he refused, saying, 'Soldier, you do your duty

and I'll do mine.' He was forcibly removed from the pulpit and replaced with a Jacobite priest, who led the prayers for James as the entire congregation – with the exception of the brave Peploe – knelt down.

22 FEBRUARY 1645 On this historic day during the Civil War, Parliamentarian Colonel Thomas Mytton of Halston took part in the successful capture of Shrewsbury. The attack in question occurred when Henry Hillier's regiment went on a foraging expedition and the Shrewsbury garrison was surprised. The attackers sawed down the wooden palisades guarding the walls and broke into the city; it is believed that traitors inside the city may have helped by opening the gates to let in a second force. They captured the governor of Shrewsbury, and rescued parliament's collector of taxes from the dungeons. The following day, the 23 February, thirteen Irish troops were hanged; the English troops were spared. In addition to his role in this capture, Mytton was vital in the storming of Wem, which had occurred the previous year on the 11 September. He then went on to capture of Oswestry, which occurred on the 23 June 1644. After this, he was made governor of the town – and ultimately the High Sherriff of Shropshire, on 30 September 1645. Mytton (59) died in the capital on 29 November 1656. His body was returned to Shrewsbury and buried in St Chad's Church, located opposite the famous Shrewsbury Quarry.

23 FEBRUARY 1927 John Thomas Giles, an Ellesmere labourer, was sentenced to death by Justice Roche for the murder of his wife on 25 November of the previous year. On the fateful day, Giles, along with his child (4), turned up at the local police station covered in blood and informed the authorities that he had just killed his wife. The officers promptly visited his house and found her in the courtyard. Amazingly, she was clinging on to life despite the long gash across her throat. Unfortunately, however, the wound was severe, and Mrs Giles died not long after.

24 FEBRUARY 1941 A flood that had persisted for sixteen days caused Shrewsbury to become nearly isolated as the river rose an amazing 18ft, the highest it had been for forty years. All main roads bar one were unusable, with some areas of the town experiencing water depths of 5ft. Pigs and sheep were drowned and, remarkably, the water reached (for the first time in years) the walls of Shrewsbury Abbey.

25 FEBRUARY 1966 On this day, Shropshire was suffering from rinderpest, an infectious viral disease otherwise known as the cattle plague. Statistics at the time showed that 3,581 cattle were infected, 2,630 of which died and 149 of which were killed. The symptoms of the disease include fever, diarrhoea and necrosis. The disease became the second in history, after smallpox, to be eradicated by human effort in 2011.

26 FEBRUARY 1945 William Henry Harris of Madeley (50) was charged with the murder of William Chaplin (79), a gamekeeper of the Apley Estate, Worfield. The incident occurred on 1 January at about 2 a.m., when the gamekeeper heard a shot erupt from the secluded wood. Suspecting that there was a poacher lurking about, Chaplin woke his son, John, and the two entered the woods in a hurry carrying only a few sticks as protection. Not long after, another shot sounded. Chaplin's son raced towards the sound, and found his father a corpse. During the trial, which was heard by Mr Justice Hilbery, Harris pled self-defence. He insisted that Chaplin had been threatening him with his stick and that he had feared for his own life. Harris was found not guilty of murder. However, he was found guilty of manslaughter, and as a result he was sentenced to seven years in prison.

27 FEBRUARY 2013 The last prisoners to be held at Shrewsbury Gaol were transferred on this day. The prison is mentioned in the famous Housman poem 'A Shropshire Lad': 'They hang us now in Shrewsbury jail / The whistles blow forlorn, / And trains all night groan on the rail / To men that die at morn.' Seven murderers were executed here during its time as a gaol. Howard Street, on which the prison stands, was named after the famous prison reformer John Howard, whose bust looks down from the prison's walls. Early in his life, Howard was captured by French

privateers and endured all the horrors of eighteenth-century prison life. This made him passionate about prison reform, and he visited prisons all over the world to report on their condition. At Shrewsbury he reported on the county gaol, county bridewell and the town gaol. In one he found an unlucky prisoner who had been sentenced to transportation five years previously but was still rotting in the cells. At the county gaol, the felons had no water and no infirmary: 'gaol fever' was therefore common. Most of the female prisoners here were pregnant, and everything had its price: even prisoners who had been found innocent at their trial had to pay 13s 4d to get out. At the country bridewell he found that conditions were even worse: 'I saw a poor creature too ill to come down the stairs; she was languishing on the floor in a consumption.' The men were kept 'in a dungeon'. Over the gate of the town gaol he noted the message, 'he that will not labour, let him not eat'. There was no sewer or water supply at this building either.

28 **FEBRUARY 1886** On this sad day William Smith ended the life of his grandchild at Bicton. The horrible event took place after the mother placed the baby in a chair near the fireplace. The chair, it turned out, was one that Smith was very particular about and thought of as his – and only his. Assuming that Smith would keep an eye on her child, the mother left the room for a matter of minutes. When she returned, she found the baby lying dead on the floor, with the base of its skull fractured and a puncture wound through its temple. Smith freely admitted to killing the child. He even helpfully informed the police that he had ended its life with the fire tongs. Smith was indicted on 9 May for the murder. During the trial his history of depression, and a family history of madness, was revealed. The jury therefore found him guilty but insane, and he was confined at His Majesty's pleasure.

29 **FEBRUARY** A popular tale from the Wrekin tells of two giants, both exiled, who decided to work together to build a new home. The brothers worked hard and piled up soil to build a massive hill, in which they left a long trench to fill up with water. This formed the River Severn. When this

first job was completed, the two exiles argued heatedly over who should get to live on the hill. One giant lost his temper and raised his spade to strike his brother over the head. Suddenly, a raven flew out of nowhere and pecked out his eyes. The spade fell down, hard, leaving a cleft in the rock. This feature is now known as Needle's Eye. The tear caused by the raven's attack became a pool, now known as Raven's Pool. The second giant then angrily knocked his brother to the ground, and buried him alive under piles of earth, leaving a mound known as the Ercall. According to local legend, if you visit the area in the middle of the night you are sure to hear the imprisoned giant groaning for help.

MARCH

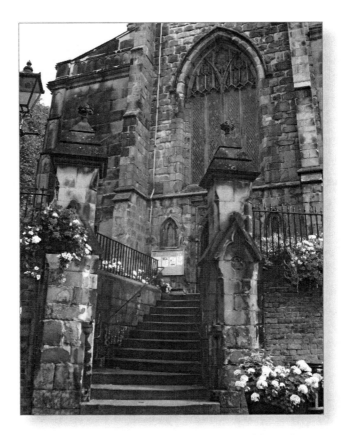

St Alkmund's Church is a 1,100-year-old Anglican
Church in the heart of Shrewsbury.
(Photo by Samantha Lyon)

1 MARCH 1945 Sergeant Joseph Stokes, a Glaswegian soldier in the King's Shropshire Light Infantry, was awarded a posthumous Victoria Cross on this date. Up until this time, Stokes' battalion had experienced a year of action and had lost 144 men, with a further 552 wounded and 66 missing in action. Stokes made three consecutive attacks on German strongpoints, and the Victoria Cross was bestowed in order to honour his bravery. On this day, in Kervenheim, his platoon came under heavy fire from a nearby farm building. Without order or instruction, Stokes navigated his way through the attack and into the building. Not long afterward, the attack came to an end and Stokes emerged from the building with five prisoners. He was remarkably steady on his feet considering that he had sustained a significant wound on his neck. This outstanding display of bravery allowed his platoon to go forward with their objectives, with an injured Stokes in tow. Despite being instructed to go back to a Regimental Aid Post, Stokes insisted on remaining with his men. He eventually succumbed to his wounds, but he kept fighting for his country right until the last minute. It was later discovered that Stokes had been badly wounded no less than eight times on the upper half of his body. It is generally agreed that without Stokes' efforts, his platoon would have experienced much greater casualties.

2 MARCH 1850 Major-General Sir Herbert Benjamin Edwardes of Frodesley, sometimes known as the 'Hero of Multan', returned from India to Shropshire on this day, which prompted an elaborate celebration amongst the Shrewsbury locals. Edwardes had recently played an important role in the second Anglo-Sikh War, ensuring a victory for the British. His return created what *The Times* reported as 'the liveliest sensations of joy and pride'. At about 3 p.m., a procession was formed in front of the Town Hall. The group marched toward the railway station in order to greet Edwardes. The streets were crowded, and Edwardes was pleasantly surprised by a congratulatory address. Later on the same year, Edwardes was awarded the honour of the degree of Doctor of Civil Law by Oxford University. This local celebrity died of pleurisy in 1868 at the young age of 49, following a significant haemorrhage. Pleurisy, once much more common and less easily treated than it is now, is a

grim disease. Essentially, it is caused when the membrane (pleura) that covers the chest cavity and lungs becomes inflamed. Symptoms include sharp and intense chest pains which are particularly noticeable when you inhale, sneeze or cough. Other famous sufferers include Benjamin Franklin and the French Queen Consort Catherine de Medici.

3   MARCH 1677 The Great Wem Fire occurred on this day. The fire began accidentally in a small house near Leek Lane when a girl by the name of Jane Churm (14) went to fetch some fuel. In the course of things, Churm absentmindedly set a twig alight with her candle – and the thatch, and afterwards the house, went up in flames. The tempestuous wind spread the fire, making it nearly impossible to put out. The climate at the time was so dry that the fire grew and spread at an alarming and destructive rate. Local topographer Revd Samuel Garbet described the fire in detail in his *History of Wem*:

> The church, the steeple, the market house, and seven score dwelling houses, besides treble the number of out-houses and buildings, were burnt. In the space of one hour they were all on fire, and the blaze was so great, that at the distance of eight or nine miles it seemed very near, and gave almost as great a light as the moon in full. In the town was a scene of the greatest confusion, and horror. The wind blustered, the flames roared, women and children shrieked. People ran at the cry of fire, to the place where it began, and at their return found their own dwellings burning. In the streets they were scorched with excessive heat, in the fields they were ready to perish with cold. Some striving to save their houses, with them lost all their goods, others despairing to extinguish the flames, attempted to carry off their most valuable effects, and many lost by thieves what they had saved from the fire; one man, and several cattle were consumed in the flames. The man was Richard Sherratt, a shoemaker ... Having fetched a parcel of shoes out of his shop, he was seen to go under the market house, which is supposed to have fallen on him.

The fire caused a horrendous amount of destruction and ultimately cost the town a great deal to repair; the damages were estimated at £23,677 3s 1d. For months after the incident, whilst rebuilding the town, people insisted that they saw a ghostly figure of a girl floating around.

Despite the fact that Wem had already seen its fair share of destruction, it had more bad luck in store. In November 1995 there was yet another fire in the area. This time the Town Hall was completely demolished by the blaze. As it was crumbling, a local sewage-farm worker by the name of Tony O'Rahilly snapped a photograph. When this photo was developed, a little girl could be seen, quite clearly, standing in the flames, behind a rail. Many believed this to be the ghost of young Jane Churm, and this photo was hailed by believers as compelling proof that ghosts exist around us. Although some photographic experts attested that the appearance of the ghost could have been caused by a trick of the light or the position of the flames, O'Rahilly went to his deathbed insisting that the picture was not fabricated. It wasn't until the year 2010 that Brian Lear (77) debunked this story by discovering an indisputable likeness between the girl in the photo and a girl on an old postcard from 1922.

In 1677, Jane Churm inadvertently caused the Great Wem Fire when she accidentally set a twig alight with her candle. (Bangin, Wikimedia Commons)

4   MARCH 1822 Mary Sandford (22) lived a short distance from Ironbridge, and had been romantically involved with Samuel Johnson (22)

for quite some time. Johnson was married, but this wasn't something that deterred him from pursuing the young woman. On 3 March, Johnson called on an excited Sandford and offered to escort her to a local dance. Sandford happily accepted. However, on the way to the venue Johnson told Sandford that he would have to go home: he claimed that he was suddenly feeling terribly ill, and that the party would make him feel worse. He asked Sandford if, instead, she would care to keep him company on a quiet walk. Sandford refused. She insisted that she go home, where a friend was waiting. Her protests were soon soothed, however, by the persuasive Johnson, who convinced her to accompany him. This was the last day Sandford was seen alive. On the 4th, Sandford's body was discovered in a shallow ditch, her mouth stuffed with hay and gagged with a silk handkerchief. The young woman had her hands tied behind her back, and bruises across her head and body. On top of these injuries, she also sported puncture wounds on her arms and head, apparently inflicted with a pitchfork that was discovered nearby. Johnson was eventually found guilty of Sandford's murder. He was hanged on the roof of Shrewsbury Prison on 30 March. His body was later sent to the Royal Salop Infirmary for dissection.

5   MARCH 1953 After Kenneth Cole (18) discovered a fire, sixty-eight visually impaired boys from the Royal Normal College for the Blind (now the Royal National) at Rowton Castle made a miraculous escape. The dormitories went up in flames early in the morning. The fire destroyed the majority of the four timber buildings that comprised the college, in addition to thirty pianos and an electric organ that were stored within. The college had to be closed and the building remained empty for many years. Eventually work began on the building to convert it into a luxury hotel. The hotel, now

known as Rowton Castle, is located a short drive from Shrewsbury town and, like many old buildings in the county, is said to be haunted. The main ghostly residents of this castle are known as the 'Blue Lady' and the 'White Lady'. Spirits known as 'White Ladies' are extremely prevalent: they usually occur in rural areas, and most are tied to terrible tragedies, usually the loss or betrayal of a loved one. They are sometimes connected with banshees, omens of death.

6   MARCH **1918** Lord Bradford of Weston Park today bought Boscobel Manor, which encompasses the historic Boscobel House. Not far from this house is the old Royal Oak that once sheltered Charles II for two days after the Battle of Worcestershire, a battle which saw the deaths of 3,000 men. Lord Bradford paid £10,000 for the property, which equates to a modern-day sum of approximately £545,800. The house was initially built as a sanctuary for Catholics in a time of need, and contains several 'priest holes' where clergy could hide. Charles II hid inside one of the holes after he'd come down from the famous oak. Some years later, in 1954, the Ministry of Works acquired the property and restored it to its nineteenth-century state. It is now in the care of the English Heritage and is fully restored.

7   MARCH **1858** Today saw the occurrence of yet another tragic mining accident. This particular incident took place in the Prior's Lee colliery in Wellington. The two victims were miners by the name of Samuel Robin (25) and Daniel Lloyd (11). The cause of the accident was an explosion of firedamp, a name given to a number of flammable gases found in coal mines. These gases have, over the years, caused a great loss of life in many coal mines. Thankfully, this came to an end with the invention of the 'Davy Lamp'. Firedamp explosions happen when the gas (methane, in most cases) collects in pockets in the coal. When these pockets are penetrated, the quick release causes massive explosions which have the potential to claim the lives of dozens of miners at a time. There were other 'damps' in the mining world, a big one being 'afterdamp' (which referred to build-up of carbon monoxide, a gas which often collects in mines after an explosion).

8 MARCH 1717 Abram Darby (39), a man who played a vital role in the Industrial Revolution, died in his Madeley Court home on this day after an eighteen-month illness. During his time, Darby came up with a method of producing pig iron in a blast furnace that could be fuelled with coke in place of charcoal, marking a significant step forward in iron production. He was buried at Broseley, and his death was followed by that of his grieving widow a few short months later. This has been known to happen when couples have been together for a significant amount of time – the phenomenon is known as 'broken heart syndrome'. Traditionally thought of as a romantic myth, it has recently been linked to a physical defect of the heart known as 'Takotsubo cardiomyopathy' or 'stress-induced cardiomyopathy'. This can be prompted by a traumatising incident, but could equally be caused by an intense shock – or indeed, by a sudden and unexpected happiness. The incident causes the brain to distribute certain chemicals that weaken the myocardium (the muscle of the heart).

9 MARCH 1919 A huge amount of damage was caused after an outbreak of fire at Ternhill Aerodrome, Market Drayton. Four Handley Pages (a type of aircraft) were destroyed, as well as a number of Avros. Thankfully, a number of machines were saved by the quick action of the officers and mechanics. This is just one example in a long list of lucky escapes for Ternhill Aerodrome. Another example can be seen seventy years after this date, on the 20 February 1989. On this date,

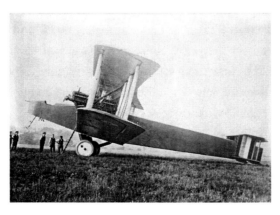

Four Handley Pages were destroyed during a fire outbreak at Ternhill Aerodrome, Market Drayton. (Library of Congress, Bain News Service, LC-DIG-ggbain-27197)

the aerodrome was attacked by two IRA bombers who set off two bombs in the accommodation barracks. Luckily, a sentry detected suspicious activity and raised the alarm, allowing the aerodrome to be evacuated and preventing otherwise certain deaths. The bombers later escaped the scene by hijacking a car from outside a local house.

10 MARCH 1898 While the King's Shropshire Light Infantry were stationed in India, a serious outbreak of the bubonic plague took place in Bombay. The ensuing panic caused by this disease soon grew out of hand and ultimately led to the sad and untimely death of two privates in the Shropshire Regiment. The bubonic plague is a disease that is mainly spread by small rodents and their fleas. The fleas infect and spread the disease by biting or scratching, thereby spreading bacteria, which quickly reproduces. Untreated, the plague kills its victim in four short days, as it did to approximately 25 million people in the fourteenth century. The first symptom of the plague, or 'Black Death' (as one particularly virulent outbreak was dubbed), is inflamed and painful lymph glands. Other grim symptoms include gangrene of the fingers, toes or other extremities, a high fever, the chills, seizures, heavy breathing, sneezing, fatigue and vomiting blood. The most disturbing thing about the plague, however, is that the pain the victim suffers during their short but intense illness is often caused by the fact that their skin is decomposing or decaying even though they are still alive ...

11 MARCH 1921 This day marked the beginning of a two-day pigeon shoot, which was arranged in order to help raise money for the Royal Salop Infirmary. Eight hundred and forty pigeons were released, and 500 were shot dead. £150 was raised, which is the equivalent of approximately £5,273 today, averaging at £6.28 per bird.

12 MARCH 1785 On this date John Green was sentenced to death for the murder of his wife, Elizabeth, who had been found shot in her cellar. It is assumed that she had been shot whilst bending over to draw beer from a barrel, as the bullet had gone straight through her head and into the drum of beer. John Green promptly put out an advertisement with an award of £50 for anyone who could provide information as to the murderer's identity. Before the murder took place, Green had left the house to watch a race with his servant – a perfect alibi. However, unknown to most at the time, at the races he had quickly informed the boy that he needed to return home to take care of 'some business'. The time it took Green to return to the racecourse would easily have allowed him to carry out the crime. When this was discovered, Green was arrested and taken to Ludlow Gaol. It was then discovered that Green's gun had been recently used, which prompted his transfer to Shrewsbury Gaol and ultimately his execution at the Old Heath on 18 March.

13 MARCH 1813 Rowland Preston was charged with the murder of Francis Bruce and Ann Taylor, and stood trial on this day. Bruce was a farmer who had slowly and diligently saved up a considerable fortune consisting of gold and silver coins, a fact that was very well known in the village. Ann Taylor, his unmarried servant, lived with him in Longford, Market Drayton. Preston had recently moved back to the area from London in order to seek work. Mr Preston dined with Farmer Bruce on the night of 18 October. He left the Bruce's house at a late hour, and on the following day the house was unusually quiet. Eventually a concerned neighbour by the name of Bradshaw crawled into the house through the roof of a cow house, after noticing that their livestock were growing hungry and learning that no one had heard from them all day. This unfortunate neighbour found Bruce and Taylor dead on the kitchen floor. Each had suffered a heavy blow to their skulls, and both had severed windpipes. During his trial Preston admitted to thieving from the house, but vehemently denied the charges of murder. He was sentenced nonetheless, and condemned to be executed on 22 March. Twenty years on, a dying man in Ellesmere, in a desperate bid to

clear his conscience, confessed to a clergyman that he had been one of the murderers, and that Preston had only stood by the door to keep watch while he and a third, unnamed member of the gang had carried out the attacks. The identity of the third man was never determined and remains a mystery.

14 MARCH 1882 On this day George Wall (53), a miner, descended a pit in Minsterley with his co-workers. As he was making his way down the ladder to begin his day of work, with a pack of black powder clinging to his chest, the candle which had afforded him a light source fell from his hat. Wall bent down to pick it up – and as he did so, the powder caught fire and exploded. The severe burns inflicted by the powder eventually killed him. Black powder was often used in mining as a means of blasting and loosening rock. The force of its explosions allowed the miners access to previously unobtainable ores and metals.

15 MARCH 1916 A motor wagon belonging to a local brewery, driving speedily over a bridge near Shrewsbury at night, derailed and landed in the Severn on this day. Thomas Evans, the driver, David Stephens, a drayman and the young Edward Rowlands were all dragged under the surface and drowned. Another youth who had been in the vehicle with them was more fortunate, as he had been thrown clear of the vehicle at impact and was able to swim to safety.

16 MARCH 1927 Local media reported on an unfortunate accident that occurred on a farm in Drenewydd (Newtown), Whittington. On this day, Harold Whitfield had a terrifying encounter with a bull which had escaped: it attacked and trampled him. Fortunately, however, his workmen were present, and they were able to beat away the bull and save Whitfield's life. He was quickly admitted to the Royal Salop Infirmary and fortunately made a recovery, as the incident could have gone very differently. Keeping bulls is a notoriously dangerous profession: they are far more muscular and aggressive than their female counterparts. They tend to weigh between 500 and 1,000kg and require very careful handling due to their temperamental nature.

17 MARCH 1828 William Perrall was a well sinker, a profession that was, more often than not, only part-time, and not very lucrative. Perrall was also a married man from Halesowen with four children. On this day, in a desperate attempt to feed his family, Perrall slipped into the home of a former employer by the name of Joseph Green. During this escapade, Perall stole bacon, a few vegetables, and an old coat. The crime was ultimately discovered by an irate Mr Green, and Perrall was soon sent off to the Shrewsbury Assizes to be tried. A guilty verdict was given to the desperate man, which at the time often meant a death penalty. Thanks to the good mood of the judge on that day, however, he was mercifully spared the noose and was instead transported for life.

18 MARCH 1792 Sarah Shenston (18) was sentenced to death on this date for the murder of her newborn baby boy, whose throat she slit immediately after his birth on the 30 September 1791. She was sentenced 'to be hanged on Thursday next and her body to be dissected and anatomized'. On the 22 March, Shenston was hanged at Moor Heath, on the outskirts of Shrewsbury.

Infanticide (or 'murder of a bastard', as it was often called at the time) was once a very common crime. At this time, in fact, it was the most common capital crime that women committed. Many hundreds of mothers killed their babies whilst experiencing severe postnatal depression. This normally happened within the first month of the baby's life. The law eventually evolved, meaning that the mother's mental state at the time of the crime could be taken into account, allowing for less draconian sentencing. With the Infanticide Act of 1922, infanticide was withdrawn at last from the list of capital crimes. Part of the Act reads, 'at the time of the act or omission the balance of her mind was disturbed by reason of her not having fully recovered from the effect of giving birth to the child or by reason of the effect of lactation consequent upon the birth of the child.' Of course, occasionally there was no insanity involved – infanticide could still be cold-hearted murder. Research into the area reveals some horrific methods, including battering, poisoning, drowning and even leaving the newborns to die in a toilet.

19 MARCH 1824 A truly vile crime was committed in this month. Richard Overfield, a labourer, was indicted at Shrewsbury Assizes on this day for the wilful murder of his three-month-old baby. The crime occurred on 21 September, and was uncovered after Overfield's wife took an emergency trip to the doctors after finding the infant suffering what seemed to be intense agony. When she kissed her baby to soothe him, she noticed that the child's lips had a remarkably sharp and acidic taste, and that his lips were white, shrivelled, and covered with blisters. Overfield, it turns out, worked in a carpet factory and so had access to sulphuric acid. This he stole to administer to the baby. The already terrible picture this forms is made all the more grotesque when you know how sulphuric acid kills: the acid is so corrosive that it burns the mouth, throat, oesophagus and stomach when ingested. It can, and often does, cause the sufferer to experience severe thirst and to have difficulty breathing. During the trial it became clear that Overfield had a significant motive, as he knew when he married his wife that she was already pregnant with another man's child.

Overfield had once told her that he would never accept the child as his own, and the court was told that he had always harboured ill-feeling towards it. After his conviction, Overfield confessed to the crime in order to purge his soul before his execution, which occurred in Shrewsbury on the 22 March.

20 MARCH 1644 During the Civil War, Sir Michael Woodhouse laid siege to Hopton Castle with 500 Cavaliers. The siege lasted a month, and the castle was only defended by twenty-eight Roundheads, who were under the command of Samuel More. On the 20 March the Royalists took the bailey and set fire to the brick tower that had been constructed by More and his garrison. Many would say that More was fooled into surrendering; he was told that the lives of his men would be spared if he stepped down. This was not to be the case, however. More's second-in-command was stabbed to death, and the rest of his men were tied up, back-to-back, before

In 1644, Sir Michael Woodhouse laid siege to Hopton Castle. (Trevor Rickard, Wikimedia Commons)

their throats were cut, and they were cast into the moat. On top of this, the Royalists reputedly attacked two maids who were in the castle at the time, killing one and wounding the other. They let the wounded maid go to tell the Parliamentarians in Herefordshire what she had witnessed, and to warn them that they would be visiting Bryan Castle next.

This tragedy saw the birth of the phrase 'Hopton quarter', which is used to describe dishonourable and treacherous action by your opponents. One particular ghostly tale claims that the twenty-eight Roundheads return to the site every year on this date.

21 MARCH 1825 The media ran a story today on a case that had demanded national attention as well as great local interest. The case was that of Capper v. Orton. On the day of the 18 March, the courtroom was full to capacity, mostly with women eager to hear the outcome. The claimant was Margaret Elizabeth Capper (18), and she was seeking compensation from Mr Robert Buckley Orton, a man seventeen years her senior, for breach of a promise of marriage. *The Times* reported that Capper desired 'reparation for the deepest injury which female youth and innocence could sustain' after Orton failed to honour their engagement. At one time, it seems, the defendant was extremely serious about making Capper, a beautiful girl from a very respectable family, his wife. Being as Orton was a wealthy gentleman of the Cheshire militia, it was generally regarded as a complimentary match, one that Capper's father was happy to allow. They met at church, where her 'charms and virtues' demanded his attention. He immediately acted, and soon rings were bought and wedding clothes purchased. Shortly before the wedding, however, Orton departed, claiming that he had some urgent business papers that required his immediate action, but promising to return the next day. A case of cold feet must have struck the scoundrel, for he failed to return. After writing a letter to the claimant's father excusing himself, the reluctant groom promptly forgot all about the engagement. In an act that provoked intense happiness from all the female onlookers, the judge rewarded a verdict of £1,000 damages for the claimant.

22 MARCH 1940 Two brothers were found dead near Minsterley. Their deaths caused great confusion at the time and remain a mystery. The brothers, Edward and Thomas, had always been close and amicable, but the evidence suggested that the pair had had a falling out: it appeared that Edward had shot his brother between the eyes from a distance of 3ft, and then turned the gun on himself. It is possible that Edward had given in to a plea made by Thomas to end his pain, as he had been suffering from an intolerable toothache for several weeks prior to his death, causing his face to swell up. According to witnesses, the pain Thomas was feeling had completely altered his usually cheery demeanour and turned him into a sullen man.

It is strange to think that even fifty-five years before this, severe dental problems could have been easily resolved by a trip to the local pharmacist. In 1885, such a problem would have been solved by 'Cocaine Toothache Drops', an anaesthetic produced by Lloyd Manufacturing that was very popular with dentists, surgeons and physicians throughout the continent. The label, which depicted wholesome children playing in a garden, declared 'take no other except Cocaine Toothache Drops, for sale by all druggists'. It wasn't until 1905 (about the same time we began using toothpaste and toothbrushes) that novocaine became the favoured form of pain relief for dentists.

23 MARCH 1812 On 1 February, a young boy discovered a dead body in a stone quarry at Redlake, Wellington. It turned out to be a retired collier by the name of William Bailey, who had been beaten up and his throat cut out. An investigation revealed that local girl Elizabeth Bowdler had seen suspicious activity the night before the discovery. Her neighbour, John Griffiths, had been seen leaving his house dragging what she described as a 'large parcel'. The police carried out a search of Griffiths' house, and found bloodstains on the floor, walls, and doorstep. They also discovered bloody sand, which had been used as an abrasive in an attempt to clean the stains from the walls. During the trial the courtroom was 'crowded to excess', and the jury was so convinced of his guilt that they took only a few minutes to return a guilty verdict. Griffiths is said to have burst into tears upon reaching his cell, where

he confessed to his crime the following day. He was executed on 23 March and sang a hymn on the scaffold before the drop.

24 MARCH 1902 On this day Clara Beatrice Lowndes (21) went into labour whilst at the home of her employer, Susannah Cooke, of Wackley Farm, Petton. For the duration of the pregnancy Lowndes had kept the truth of her condition from her employer; even when Cooke got suspicious and asked her outright whether or not she was with child Lowndes firmly denied the accusation. She knew that a pregnancy would put her out of work. When she complained of a stomach ache, therefore, she was given some painkillers and told to go back to bed. When Cooke saw Lowndes later on, in the outhouse, she noticed blood on her clothing. This sparked further discussion of pregnancy – which Lowndes once again denied. The painkillers, she claimed, had been responsible for the blood. Cooke later discovered what looked like a baby in the outhouse, and promptly contacted the police. The servant was found guilty of concealing a birth. However, as her mental state at the time of the crime was called into question – it being suspected that she was not able, at the time, to realise or to understand what she was doing – she was not found guilty of murder. She was subsequently sentenced to six months in prison.

25 MARCH 1821 More than 500 miners gathered together in Dawley on 2 February 1821 for a protest march against wage reductions. As the miners marched on they grew in numbers and eventually totalled over 3,000 men. After a violent encounter with the local Yeomanry, two men died and many others were injured, resulting in much ill-feeling in the area. This conflict took place on the Cinder Hills and Old Park, north of Dawley, and accordingly the riots came to be known as 'The Battle of Cinderloo'. Following this event, many protesters were arrested and jailed. Nine of the prisoners were tried before the Shrewsbury Assizes on this day. Thomas Palin was convicted of the capital crime of 'felonious assault' and so hanged in Shrewsbury on the 7 April. Although Samuel Hayward was also convicted, he was fortunately reprieved on 2 April. The remainder were imprisoned

Thomas Palin was convicted of the capital crime of felonious assault and was hanged in Shrewsbury on 7 April 1821. (THP)

for nine months. Following Palin's execution, the *Salopian Journal* stated its desire that 'the returning good sense and right feelings of our working population in the recently disturbed parts of the County will forever render unnecessary the repetition of so awful an example'.

26 MARCH 1823 On this day farmer John Newton (40) was executed for the murder of his wife, Sarah, who at the time was six months pregnant with her fifth child. The crime took place at their home in Severn Hall, Bridgnorth, after George Edwards (a local brazier and tin-plate worker) stopped by Newton's house with a bill for 3s. Newton was outraged, as he claimed that he had already given his wife the money to settle the debt. He let Edwards know, in no uncertain terms, that his wife would be thrashed for her failure to pay, as she had to be taught a lesson. This wasn't the first time she had driven him into debt, he said. Edwards begged him not to do anything rash, saying that he would rather forget the debt altogether and that it was ridiculous to cause so much trouble over such a small amount

of money. Edwards stayed for a beer or two. He did not leave until Newton promised that he would not hurt his wife. Newton finally relented, but the following day he showed up on Edwards' doorstep looking for the local doctor, claiming that, 'a bad job has happened', and that his wife was suffering with a pregnancy-related problem. However, as it came out in court, this was not the case: Newton had beaten his wife so violently that the true extent of her injuries could not be described during the trial. One of his children, who tried to protect his mother, might also have been a victim but was thankfully spry enough to outrun his father. When Newton was eventually convicted of the murder he is known to have said, with some disbelief, 'I have lost my life for three shillings.'

27 MARCH 1914 An inquest was held on the body of Revd David Wigley Abbott, the vicar of Cardington. He had been found dead on the 25th near his vicarage, with a bullet wound through his head. A search of the vicarage revealed a note that read, 'Another sleepless night. No real sleep for weeks. Oh, my poor brain! I cannot bear the lengthily dark hour of the night. Dazed, confused, I know not what I am doing. God have mercy on me and raise up friends to my poor wife.' A verdict of suicide during temporary insanity was returned. Suicide by a man of the cloth would have been considered very shocking at the time, as laws against suicide were developed from religious doctrine – God, and only God, it was felt, had the right to decide when people should die. As such, suicide was a crime against God. Suicide became illegal in the 1200s, and until the 1800s your possessions would be offered to the Crown (rather than your family) if you committed suicide. It wasn't until the Suicide Act of 1961 that suicide and attempted suicide stopped being a criminal offence.

28 MARCH 1888 William Arrowsmith of Denton was executed on this day for the murder of his uncle, George Pickerill (80). The crime occurred on the 11 November 1887 on a visit to his uncle's house, who lived in a small cottage in Lower Prees, near Whitchurch. Arrowsmith brutally beat his uncle and slit his throat. He then stole some of his possessions, along

with some of his money. Pickerill's body was discovered on 12 November by his daughter, who often came around to clean and cook. When she found him he was in the kitchen with twelve wounds across his face and head. A blood-stained butcher's knife was found nearby. Arrowsmith was arrested after he was seen, rather unwisely, selling the stolen goods. The police were eventually able to secure the conclusive evidence they required using a very basic form of forensic science, when they matched his footprints to those found at the crime scene. By this time, public executions were no longer held, but over 500 spectators congregated outside the prison on this day to watch the black flag being hoisted over the porter's lodge, which signalled that Arrowsmith's life had been brought to a close.

29 MARCH 1834 Shropshire's most popular and well-known eccentric, John 'Mad Jack' Mytton (37) of Halston Hall died on this day, paralysed, bloated, and heavily in debt. He certainly squeezed a lot into his young life. His father died when John was only two, and his wealthy mother spoiled him extensively to compensate. For Mytton, life appeared to be mostly a challenge to find more and more creative and insane ways to blow his inheritance. During his time he kept 2,000 dogs, which he fed on steak and champagne. He had a habit of leaving huge bundles of cash in hedges, or buried around his estate. It did not take long for him to squander his considerable inheritance and acquire a huge debt, meaning he had to flee the country for fear of being sent to gaol. In order to properly stress the peculiarity of his character, you would have to know that he enjoyed hunting naked with his pet monkey and that he once threw his wife's lapdog on the fire and set fire to his own nightshirt to cure his hiccups. Mytton also dressed up as a highwayman one day in order to chase his friends, whom he shot at as they ran for their lives.

30 MARCH 1867 This date marks a terrible death from exposure in the harsh Shropshire weather. The incident occurred near Chirbury, on the border of Shropshire and Wales. Thomas and Vincent Preece met in an inn at Stapeley Hill. The deceased, Thomas, was visiting his brother.

Shortly after 8 p.m., the brothers left the inn and set off in the heavy snow and the freezing cold for Chirbury. Halfway across the hill, Vincent turned to his brother – only to note he was no longer there. He called for him, but the wind rendered further shouting futile. Assuming his brother had gone on ahead of him, he set off once again. It took him four hours to walk the usually short trip home, and when he finally arrived everyone was in bed. The next morning, when it became clear that Thomas was not home, Vincent sent his son off in search of him. After only a quick search, the youngest Preece found his uncle's body, face down in the snow. The inquest claimed that he must have fallen down from exhaustion and gone to sleep. Thomas had known the area very well, which only goes to show how drastic a winter it was.

31 MARCH 1832 James Lea and Joseph Grindley were executed for arson after they set fire to a stack of barley belonging to John Nunnerley of Whitchurch on 12 September 1831. For a long time there existed more than 200 capital offences in the UK, the number having grown since the reign of King Henry VIII. King George oversaw an increase of sixty further capital offenses. After growing concern, the Reform Act of 1832 caused the ultimate punishment to be removed from almost two thirds of the capital crimes that once existed. Unfortunately, Lea and Grindley were not quite in time for this legal reformation.

APRIL

St Mary's Church, Shrewsbury.
(Photo by Samantha Lyon)

1 APRIL, 1863 Edward Cooper (30), a labourer from Baschurch, was executed on this day for the murder of his son, John (8), marking the first public hanging in Shrewsbury for nine years. Cooper was a widower and father of two. His daughter, Jane, lived with and worked for a friend of the family. The crime occurred the previous December in Hanwood, and during the trial it became clear that Cooper's personality was not entirely stable. He had implored the help of a fellow labourer, Thomas Jones, to look after his child, as he was not able to cope. He told Jones that if he did not help he would hang the boy and then himself. Evidence showed that on the fateful day John had accompanied Cooper to a coppice, where Cooper often went hunting for rabbits. In an attempt to cleanse his conscience, Cooper admitted in the days leading up to his execution that he had strangled the boy with a handkerchief – whilst his victim begged him to stop – and that he had no idea why he committed the crime. After the deed was done, Cooper visited one Mary Abbot to borrow a spade, and buried his son at the scene of the crime. He was regularly to return to the site in order to hunt and 'did not feel much about it [the crime]'. When the locals noticed John's absence, Cooper insisted that the boy was staying with his grandmother and would remain there indefinitely. The inquest, which was held at the Duncan Inn in Baschurch, showed that the child's tongue had swollen and protruded through the teeth. At the inquest, the face of the poor boy was seen to have decomposed so badly that it was unrecognisable. The only way they were able to identify the child was due to a deformity. On the night before his hanging, Cooper is reported to have slept soundly. He had a large appetite in the morning and even made small talk about the weather. As his final moments arrived, though, he finally seemed to grasp the reality of his situation and began to cry. His last words were, 'Oh Lord, bless my soul! God bless you all.' Approximately 10,000 people attended the execution – brilliantly demonstrating the morbid fascination with murder which mankind is prone to.

2 APRIL, 1842 This day marks the execution of John Williams, a well-known criminal from Wrexham. On the day of his hanging the English and

On the day of John Williams' execution, the Welsh Bridge was crammed full of eager spectators. (Photo by Samantha Lyon)

Welsh bridges were crammed full, meaning that anyone wanting to travel through on their carriages was out of luck. The crime that he swung for was the murder of Emma Evans, a lady who lived alone and ran a successful shop in Bronygarth. One day Williams, along with another man named William Slawson, convinced Evans to let them in after closing time to buy tobacco. Their real intentions became clear after she opened the door, however: they knocked her on the head, cut her throat and ransacked the place. Slawson had a good lawyer and managed to plead to a lesser charge of robbery, for which he received seven years' transportation. Williams was not so lucky. His body was buried on prison grounds near the Beckbury Butcher, and his head was cast in plaster of Paris by the Coalport China Manufactory.

3   APRIL 1819 John Denny (64) was executed at Shrewsbury for stabbing and attempting to murder John Wilde of Pontesbury, a reverend with a wife and one son. It was revealed in court that Denny had stabbed Wilde

when the vicar refused him readmission to the Pontesbury Workhouse on the basis that he had sufficient money and wasn't in desperate need. An aggrieved Denny struck out at Wilde. The wounded man did not, at first, realise that he had been stabbed: it was only when he went to sit down and felt his jacket filling up with warm blood that the realisation dawned. He left the room, shouting, 'Murder!' Denny was immediately detained. Thankfully, Revd Wilde recovered from his injuries.

4 APRIL, 1829 John Evans, alias Squire Smallman, was executed for the murder of Edward Richards and was subsequently buried by his family in St Mary's Church. The crime occurred outside a public house at Bishop's Castle on 20 February. At the time, Evans was wanted for – amongst other crimes – a burglary at Woodmington. When Evans entered the pub and asked for a beer, the landlord immediately recognised the fugitive. So did Richards, who was in the pub at the time. Richards followed Evans into the pub's garden to confront him. Presumably in an attempt to disguise himself, Evans was dressed in a blue gown, from which he withdrew a gun and shot Richards in the chest. Richards collapsed, and died not long afterwards. Although Evans escaped, he was found and arrested shortly afterwards: he returned to the scene of the crime early the next morning to search for his gun, which he had lost during the scuffle with his victim.

Squire Smallman was buried in St Mary's graveyard following his execution. (Photo by Samantha Lyon)

5 **APRIL, 1822** Samuel Whitehouse of Halesowen died on this day after forty-eight hours of suffering, the result of a terrible blow to the head. It was supposedly inflicted by his brother-in-law and neighbour Joseph Downing, with whom he had always been on very good terms. During the trial the facts of the case were revealed to the public. Whitehouse and Downing, it seemed, had gone to the house of a blacksmith named Thomas Fox on 3 April, as they planned to indulge in their mutual hobby of hunting wildfowl. After taking their fill of shooting, the three men retired for a drink in the local pub. Afterwards, they mounted their horses and left for the woods, the shortest way home. A short way into the woods, however, Downing said that he had forgotten something at Fox's house and turned back. Soon after, the remaining two parted ways, and Whitehouse's horse was found wandering through the woods in 'a state of eye-rolling terror' by a young boy, who subsequently sought help. Whitehouse was found in the wood soon afterwards, knocked unconscious and left for dead. His money and pocket watch had been taken. The stricken man was returned to his home and tended to by a doctor, but unfortunately his injuries were too severe to survive, and he passed away shortly afterwards. Though Downing was offering a reward for any information about Whitehouse's killer, he himself was then accused of the murder.

The prosecution claimed that Downing, who had been frosty towards Whitehouse on the day in question, had bashed him on the back of the head with a gun barrel. Remarkably, during the trial the defence suggested that the victim's horse had been scared by a ghost, the existence of which was generally accepted and believed in the area. Evidence from two doctors regarding the likelihood of the victim's injuries being consistent with being thrown off a saddle and crushed by a hoof was compelling enough to sway the verdict. Downing, who had been the picture of composure during the trial, broke down into fits of tears when a verdict of 'not guilty' was returned, and thanked the jury. The real murderer, if there had in fact been one, was never convicted.

6 **APRIL, 1833** William Handley was executed for the attempted murder of gamekeeper John Bannock, whom he and John Handley had shot at three

times, with one shot going right through his eye. Both men were tried for the crime, but William Handley alone was found guilty. The judge who sentenced him said at the trial, 'It is a most heinous offence ... attempting to destroy the life of a fellow creature. It makes me sick to tell a young man like you, in the bloom of health and in the figure of youth that your life must atone for the offence you have committed.' A writer for the *Salopian Journal* said of the trial, 'His fate should be a warning to those numerous desperadoes who have for some time infested this and other counties, and so often added to the crowded state of our prisons, and who, pursuing the profitless and dangerous practice of poaching, are led on, step by step, to the commission of other crimes, and until, as in the present instance, their lives become ... forfeited to the offended laws of their country.'

7   APRIL, 1854   John Lloyd was executed on this day for the murder of John Griffins. It was revealed in court that Griffins had accused Lloyd, a lodger at his home, of carrying on an affair with his wife and of being the real father of his newborn baby. Whether he was genuinely insulted or reacting out of a guilty conscience, Lloyd got angry and threatened a 'good lancing' if his landlord repeated the accusation. He left the house to regain his composure, but the next day he returned with a gun, which he aimed through the kitchen window. Griffin received most of the lead shot in his head, as he was bending down to tie his laces, but strangely enough refused to get help for a few hours, insisting that he was fine. He died in the Royal Salop Infirmary ten days after receiving the wound. Lloyd's execution was a popular one, and the Dana steps had to be barricaded as there were worries that the combined weight of the gathered onlookers would make them collapse.

8   APRIL, 1852   News broke on an inquest that was held a number of days before at the Bridgnorth Union Workhouse on the body of John Gitton (50), who was found murdered on 29 March. Henry Lewis Colley was subsequently charged with the murder. Colley came to the workhouse on 9 January from Shrewsbury's lunatic asylum, and the inquest revealed that

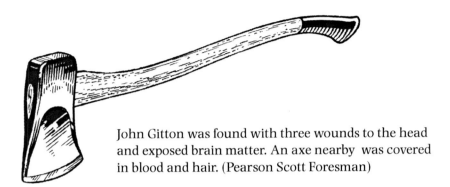

John Gitton was found with three wounds to the head and exposed brain matter. An axe nearby was covered in blood and hair. (Pearson Scott Foresman)

for a few minutes on the day in question, the two men were left in a room together, with only a blind boy as a witness (who could give no account of what happened). Gitton died from three wounds to the head, the skull having been so broken in three places that the brains were exposed. Nearby an axe that was covered with hair, blood and brains was found. When the alarm was sounded, Colley got up to leave the boardroom, where the master was reading prayers. He was found a few hours later in town, with bloodstains on his trousers. He insisted that he was given permission to leave and denied any knowledge of the murder.

9   APRIL, 1868   This day saw the public execution of John Mapp (35), who was found guilty of murdering Catherine Lewis (9), the youngest of five children. Mapp had returned from Australia after having served out a term of transportation for assaulting an old woman. The appearance of Catherine's bloodied hat three days before Christmas Day prompted a search in the quiet farming village of Longden. Her father discovered her body in a small hut, with a 5in wound to her throat. Her devastated father noticed that a glass and brass brooch that her step-mother had gifted and pinned on before Catherine went missing had disappeared. Mapp's house was searched and the brooch was found in his coat pocket. Bloodstains were discovered on his trousers and coat, along with a blood-stained knife. Mapp was arrested on Christmas Eve and tried before Sir Fitzroy Kelley.

(Before Kelley became a judge, he was perhaps the highest paid and most successful barrister of the Victorian age. He earned the nickname 'Apple-Pip Kelly' after he successfully convinced a jury that a woman died of eating too many apples rather than of swallowing acid.) Following the trial, the jury were locked in a room 'without meat or drink, fire or candle' until they came to a decision. The jury took only six minutes to decide his fate. On the day of his execution, at a 7.45 a.m., Mapp was handed over to his executioner, the famous William Calcraft. He was unusually calm and composed, slight trembling aside. When the time came, he shook Calcraft's hand and said goodbye, but as the drop fell he turned his head, meaning that the rope was displaced and caught around his chin rather than his neck. This caused his death to be comparatively prolonged: he struggled, in agony, for thirty seconds before he died. Mapp was the fourth-to-last person to be publically hanged in the UK, as public hanging was abolished on 29 May of this year.

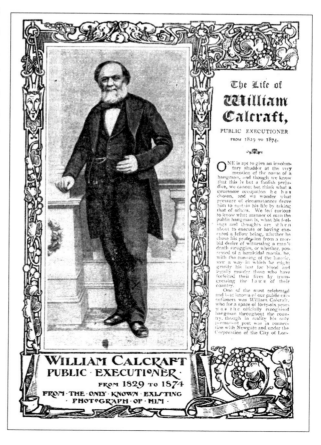

John Mapp was executed by William Calcraft, the famous hangman. (THP)

10 APRIL, 1899 There is no shortage of mining-related accidents in Shropshire's history, and today saw another unfortunate example. The collier injured today, who went by the name of Thomas Hopwood (39), was a worker at the Donnington Grange Colliery. This time the accident was caused by a fall, which caused the unfortunate Hopwood a significant back injury. The injury turned out to be so severe that it caused paralysis and further health problems developed. The miner made it to the twentieth century, but died on 23 January 1900.

11 APRIL, 1788 Thomas Deakin, informer, was fined and given a prison sentence of one year in Shrewsbury Gaol for defrauding Elizabeth Matthews. On this day Deakin was also instructed to stand in the pillory in Shrewsbury square for two hours and to pay a fine of £10, the equivalent of roughly £1,240. In this era, the pillory was a much-feared sentence: during their time restrained within the pillory, members of the public would usually throw things at the criminal – and victims could, and did, die of injuries caused by the crowd's missiles, which typically included stones, filth and dead animals. The device is similar to the stocks, save that the prisoner is left standing. It was often used to humiliate and to provoke public ridicule, with the hope of deterring potential criminals from committing similar crimes. It consisted of a wooden post that trapped the prisoner, with holes for the neck and wrists.

12 APRIL, 1600 On this day, another man was fixed into the pillory. Around his neck was a note that explained that he had been judged guilty of attempting to murder Thomas Onslow of Boreatton, his employer. The pillory, as a form of punishment, was eventually abolished in 1837.

13 APRIL, 1546 Alice Glaston (11) was hanged on this day along with two other prisoners. She may have been the youngest girl ever to be hanged in England. She was buried in Much Wenlock. Unfortunately, the Quarter Sessions' records for this time have not survived the years, and as such the crime that she was hanged for is unknown. What is known is that she would have been tried at Wenlock Guildhall, which was built in 1540, and she would have gone to Edge Top to be hanged. She was later buried in the parish church and her burial was recorded by Sir Thomas Botelar, a vicar in the area. As shocking as this execution is, John Dean was still younger when he was executed for arson at Abingdon Assizes. On 23 February 1629, Dean was hanged by the neck until dead when he was only 8 years old.

14 APRIL, c. 800 A well-known tale that the Wrekin inspired is that of Gwendol the giant (occasionally substituted in the tale by the Devil). According to the local legend, Gwendol Wrekin ap Shenkin ap Mynyddmawr held a grudge against Shrewsbury, and decided that he wanted to bring an end to the town and everyone in it. Gwendol grabbed his spade, and an equally massive amount of earth, and set off towards Shrewsbury. When he reached Wellington he met a cobbler who was on his way back from Shrewsbury market with a sack full of shoes, slung over his shoulder, for repair. Gwendol stopped to ask for the directions and the quick-witted cobbler, suspecting something was amiss, asked the giant what he wanted to go to Shrewsbury for. He soon learned of the giant's vengeful plan. The cobbler then told the giant that it was in fact a very long way, and emptied the sack of shoes onto the ground, saying that he had worn out every one of the shoes on his walk back. Obviously deciding the task was not worth the effort it would cost him, the giant dropped the earth on the ground beside him and went home. This, according to legend, is how the Wrekin was formed. Just to add to the tale, some also say that when the giant scraped mud off his large boots it created the nearby Ercall Hill.

15 APRIL, 1816 On this day, *The Times* reported on the crime committed by an 'S. Franks', who was tried for the wilful murder of his elderly

father at Cardigan. The principal witness was an apprentice farmer, who recalled that, on the day in question, the deceased had struck his wife on her face in the presence of the prisoner, who then took up a thatching stick and beat his father until he fell down. The injuries the son inflicted were so severe that the father died soon afterwards. Luckily for the prisoner, however, the surgeon who examined the father's skull told the court that the deceased might have been killed by the fall, rather than the beating. Franks was therefore found guilty of manslaughter and imprisoned for a year.

16 APRIL, 1914 The home of Sir Walter Smyth, Acton Burnell Hall, was nearly demolished by an outbreak of fire, leaving only the walls standing. Thankfully the fire brigades got there in time to save the Roman Catholic chapel that was adjoined, and the majority of the Acton Burnell pictures. The hall was rebuilt the following year and is now home to Concord College, an international private school.

17 APRIL, 1873 On this day a miner by the name of Mr Morrall was crushed to death in the Ketley Colliery in Wellington, after a 'fall of the roof' landed on top of him. Unfortunately, accidents like this were all too common in the mining trade, which is always a risky profession. Due to the long hours that were required, the manual labour and the attention required, workers were often exhausted. When people were overworked to this extent, fatal mistakes became much more likely to occur.

18 APRIL, 1919 An inquest began in North Shropshire on the body of John Williams, a farmer in Kynaston Farm, Kinnerley. After the inquest, James Rogers Treginford, another farmer, was officially charged with manslaughter at Oswestry Police Court.

19 APRIL, 1777 At the then traditional hanging site of Old Heath, Jeffery Williams was hanged for the crimes of 'horse stealing and house breaking'. It is believed that the gallows at this location was simply a large tree.

The criminal in question would be transferred to the location on a cart and, after he had a noose placed appropriately, the cart would be moved away – leaving the criminal choking at the end at the rope. The crimes of 'horse stealing and house breaking' remained capital offences until 1830, when Lord John Russell abolished the death sentence for these crimes (along with many others).

20 APRIL, 1823 On this day the people of Lilleshall noted an odd chemical phenomenon near Lilleshall Coal Works, on a field belonging to Mrs Brigden of Muckston. The field had been drained days earlier, and when some gentlemen in the neighbourhood were walking along the earth they noted a crackling noise. They presumed it was water, but it turned out to be carbonated hydrogen gas. This gas has a rotten odour and is not altered or absorbed by water. It is extremely flammable and, when lit, burns with a deep, thick bluish flame. When a flame was applied, the earth blazed, incredibly but temporarily. For quite a while, until the vapour dissipated, people in the neighbourhood kept visiting to relight the field and watch the sparks fly.

21 APRIL, 1919 Local media reported the death of Harold Evison (17), from Northwood, who shot himself in a field on 19 April. The suicide was apparently carried out during a fit of temporary insanity set off by worry, after his sister had enquired about whether he knew anything about £5 that she was missing. This would be a modern-day equivalent of approximately £220.

22 APRIL, 1933 William Thomas Wootton of Bishops Castle was charged with the manslaughter of his daughter, Mavis Annie Wootton (8 months). On the day in question, Wootton threw a table knife at a nearby partition. Tragically, the knife instead ended up piercing the infant's skull. According to Wootton, the death was the result of 'pure accident': he had thrown the knife, in a fit a pique, after losing his temper during a family dispute. He was ultimately found not guilty.

23 APRIL, 1936 Dorothy Clewes (18) died on this day from a tetanus infection, the result of being shot by a farm labourer named Ernest Robert Hill. Both were inhabitants of Moreton Say. Hill had once been Clewes' boyfriend, but she broke up with him, much to his dismay, after a heated argument. He was a paranoid and jealous sort, a trait exacerbated by the fact that Clewes, a popular and outgoing girl, tended to draw a lot of male attention. On Easter Monday, 13 April, Hill saw Clewes wearing eye-catching clothes and make-up and became angry. Later that day, about 1.5 miles from Market Drayton, Hill was cycling when he saw Clewes with her sister, Florrie, and a friend named Phyllis Garrett. When Hill passed them he cast a cold look in her direction but pedalled on. Not long after, however, he stopped his bicycle, dismounted, and began to wait, leaning on a nearby fence. When the girls passed him, he stalked into the centre of the road to stop them, his hand obscured underneath his coat. Clewes greeted Hill amicably, but before the girls knew what was happening the man had produced a small shotgun and pressed it to Clewes' dress. Clewes, desperate to calm him, told him not to be silly and to let them walk on by, but before she could make her escape Hill had pulled the trigger, shooting her in her left arm. He then put the gun back in his pocket, mounted his bicycle, and headed on. Clewes was taken to the Royal Salop infirmary, where her condition slowly deteriorated. Originally the wound was relatively superficial, but tetanus developed, with tragic results. Even more tragically, if tetanus had been anticipated then the young girl might have lived. When brought to trial, on 27 June, Hill was convicted of manslaughter. The charge would have been murder, but due to his questionable mental state at the time of the shooting – and the fact that he insisted he had only intended to wound the girl – a lesser charge was found. As a result, Hill served only three years in prison for his crime.

24 APRIL, 1887 Today saw another tragic firedamp related mining accident. Meredith (48), a miner, passed away on this day when the gas was unintentionally lit by a lamp and exploded.

25 APRIL, 1879 On this day, the miner John Corfield (27) fell to his death while working in the Roman Gravels Colliery. He fell a total of 82m down the new south engine shaft and died on impact.

26 APRIL, 1646 On the 1 April of this year, Royalist troops set fire to the houses in Bridgnorth High Street with the hope of hampering the Parliamentarians. This fire grew and spread rapidly to the surrounding buildings, eventually reaching St Leonard's Church which was being used, at the time, as Cromwell's gunpowder store. This created a massive explosion that burned almost all of Bridgnorth High Street to the ground. More than 300 families were made homeless and penniless due to the fire. On this day, the town was surrendered to Parliament. Cromwell later gave orders for the castle to be torn down, which was done by 1647: only remnants of the castle now exist. Stone was taken from this fallen castle and used to help repair Bridgnorth's destroyed buildings.

Cromwell gave orders for the Bridgnorth Castle to be torn down, and today only remnants of the castle remain. (Brian Voon Yee Yap, Wikimedia Commons)

27 APRIL, 1925 Local newspapers reported that, for the first time ever, an aeroplane was used as a hearse when George Powell, who had been killed in a motor accident, was flown from Croydon Aerodrome to the Shrewsbury Aerodrome for his funeral and subsequent burial at Stanton.

28 APRIL, 1952 Sir John Bayley, the first headmaster and founder of Wellington College (now known as Wrekin College) died on this day at the grand age of 99.

29 APRIL, 1953 A verdict of suicide was returned following the inquest of the death of Revd Ivor Kirkham (39), the curate of Pontesbury. It seems that he shot himself on the 26th when 'the balance of the mind was disturbed'. He was discovered by his unfortunate wife in his study with a gunshot wound through his head. A rifle was found nearby.

When Revd Ivor Kirkham's body was discovered, a rifle was found nearby.

30 APRIL, 1139 King Stephen moved from Worcester onto Ludlow to besiege the castle. At this time Lady Marion de la Bruyere lowered a rope for Arthur, her secret love, so that he could climb up to her tower. Unfortunately for the enamoured Marion, she was betrayed by her lover, who was an enemy of Ludlow. As Arthur did his best to distract her, he very deliberately and sneakily left the rope hanging down below for the castle's enemies to climb. In no time at all, 100 of his men had climbed the rope and invaded the castle. Upon discovering this, Marion became outraged and stabbed her lover with his own sword. Then, filled with shame and guilt, she jumped from the Pendover Tower, dying on impact with the ground. Although this may be romantic conjecture, many attest

that her last words were 'goodbye, cruel world!' Many also firmly believe that her ghost, who is generally known as 'Marion of the Heath', re-enacts the tragedy nightly, and that if you stand by the tower at night you can hear her screaming. Ludlow Castle features in the story 'FulkFitzWarin', and the Marion-Arthur romance is believed by some to be the inspiration for the Robin Hood legend.

The tragic romance between Lady Marion de la Bruyere and Arthur is believed by some to be the inspiration for the Robin Hood legend. (Vasa1628, Wikimedia Commons)

MAY

The famous doorway to the Dingle within the quarry,
Shrewsbury, which is believed by some to be haunted
by a Mrs Foxall. (Photo by Samantha Lyon)

1   MAY 1874   William Henry Foulke of Dawley was a professional sportsman who was known for his height (6ft 4in) and build (24 stone). He died on this day at the age of 42. His death certificate cites 'cirrhosis' as the cause of death. Cirrhosis is a chronic liver disease and is characterised by the liver tissue being replaced by nodules and scar tissue. This eventually leads to liver failure and death.

2   MAY 1860   On this day William Brindley, a railway company employee, was driving the passenger train from Shrewsbury to Crewe. When Brindley approached Whitchurch a goods train appeared from the opposite direction of the single line. The trains collided, causing the death of Mr John Jones. Brindley was thereby brought before the court on a charge of manslaughter. It was claimed that he had caused the death of Jones through gross negligence, as he failed to take note of a danger signal that a porter had sounded. He was found guilty but was only sentenced to one year in prison.

In 1860, John Jones was killed when a passenger train and a goods train collided at Shrewsbury Station, seen here in 1962. (Ben Brooksbank, Wikimedia Commons)

3   MAY 1782 Mary Davies, who kept a little shop in the village of
Dorrington, was murdered on this day by her lodger Sarah Turner (alias
Marygold), who strangled her and then broke her head open with a coal
axe. The facts, as they were later revealed in court, were that Davies wanted
her lodger to wake up at 8 a.m., but Turner refused, claiming she was
tired. The lodger did eventually get up, however, and went downstairs to
where the older woman was. Here, Turner took her landlady by surprise
by wrapping a cord tightly around her neck several times. She stopped this
assault when she believed her victim was dead. However, Davies wasn't yet
completely defeated, and was able to recover enough to beg for her life. By
this point, however, it was too late: Sarah was so frightened that she would
be turned in that she dragged Davies to the coalhouse and ended her life
with the axe. After this vile deed, she robbed the shop of £7. When the shop
wasn't opened at the usual time, some of the regulars investigated. They
found the back door ajar, let themselves in and found Mary on the floor with
brain matter leaking out of her skull. Turner was found guilty by the jury,
tried for murder and executed for the crime on 29 July.

4   MAY 1922 Local media announced the upcoming visit of Henri Mathias
Berthelot, the French general, who was set to visit Shrewsbury on 3 June
to pin the Croix de Guerre to the colours of the 4th Battalion of the King's
Shropshire Light Infantry. This honour was awarded due to their brave
conduct at Bligny on 5 June 1918. At the time they were serving with the
French Fifth Army, commanded by General Berthelot, when they helped in
the vital retake of Bligny Hill from the Germans and suffered nearly 100
casualties.

5   MAY Shropshire abounds with folklore. In the hills surrounding
Church Stretton roams, according to rumour, a large hound whose eyes
glow bright red. The dog is supposed to be a manifestation of Eadric the
Wild, the local hero who raised a resistance to the Norman Conquest
and allied himself to the Welsh prince of Gwynedd. At Bomere Heath,
local legend attests that in a pool there are large magical fish protecting a

sword that was planted in the water-bed long ago. The sword is meant to belong to Wild Eadric, and the tale bears a resemblance to the legend of King Arthur, as the fish will only give the sword away once its true heir, or Eadric himself, returns to wield it.

6 MAY 1875 On this day Arthur Allen Morris and Jane Mason, his mother's servant, planned to officialise their long-standing affection by tying the knot in Liverpool. Mason was in her room, excitedly preparing for the day ahead, when Morris knocked on the door and asked whether she was ready. She told him she would be just a little longer, so he left – but returned thirty minutes later, insisting that he be let in 'for a talk'. Relenting, Mason opened the door to him, and Morris led her to another room where he subjected her to a series of bizarre, incoherent questions. He asked who she was, and what her name was, before suddenly striking her on the head. Worse, he then produced a knife, with which he stabbed Mason several times in various places. Two wounds were particularly vicious, one stab penetrating a lung and the other lancing right through her cheek and into her mouth. After his attack came to an end, Morris went downstairs for some whisky and a cigar.

During the subsequent trial, the defence did not try to dispute the violence of the attack, but only said that due to drink: the groom had not been in his right mind. The judge asked the jury to consider if the defendant was insane at the time he committed the assault. This was an interesting – if extremely gruesome – case, as an important legal question was posed: could inebriation be recognised as a legal defence? It could not: the jury decided that Morris had no excuse for his actions, and found him guilty of unlawfully wounding Mason with intent to murder. If they had decided differently, the precedent would have had an interesting but frightening effect on criminal law.

7 MAY 1867 A rail accident occurred on this day on the Severn Valley railway between Shrewsbury and Worcester. A passenger train left Worcester and, when nearing Bridgnorth, abruptly and unexpectedly derailed. It dragged behind it two carriages, which travelled for

approximately 90m, tearing up the rails on the way. The train finally came to a halt when the engine and two carriages fell onto their sides. Miraculously, no one was killed during the accident, although the stoker was very badly injured.

8 MAY 1854 A boy of 13 was admitted to the Reformatory for Juvenile Criminals at Saltley, following a request from the Shropshire magistrates. The boy had already had two stays at the Shrewsbury Prison for felony and came from a family that suffered many hardships following the death of his father. His mother had remarried, but the happy marriage suffered as her husband delved into a life of crime and was transported for seven years. This proved to be too much for the boy's mother, who couldn't bear the pressure and abandoned her children. The boy's older brother had been in prison three times and was then also transported. His sister became a convicted thief and prostitute in a desperate attempt to support her family. The felonious behaviour reached to their extended family, as well, and their cousin (10) was sent to prison twice and another cousin (16) three times.

9 MAY 1951 Officer Cadet T.S. Murphy of Ternhill RAF station was killed on this day in Boscobel after his trainer aircraft crashed and burst into flames.

10 MAY 1709 In the church of Astley Abbotts, north of Bridgnorth, there exists the remains of a 'maiden's garland'. The garland is a heart-shaped frame, made of wood and decorated with cloth and ribbons. It exists in loving memory of Hannah Phillips, who drowned on this day while crossing the River Severn on the day before her wedding. She had been on the way back from helping with final preparations for the following day. People say that her ghost, 5ft tall and wearing a long dark dress and a shawl, has been seen by motorists on Broseley road to Bridgnorth. She has become a tragic symbol, as some say she keeps making the same journey each night, preparing for a wedding that will never take place.

11 MAY 1891 In late April of this year, influenza became an epidemic in London for the second time. Soon after, this epidemic spread to other parts of the UK. By May, it had hit Shrewsbury hard and a great number of people were taken to hospital and dispensaries in order to be treated. On this day Charles George Wingfield (58) of Onslow Hall, who had been a colonel of the Shropshire Yeomanry for many years, died from the infectious disease.

12 MAY 1914 Edward Thomas Williams was killed in a car accident near Shrewsbury on this day. He was driving a car from London to Powis Castle and had stopped to invite five men and one woman for a ride. Early in the morning, as they were speeding along, they crashed into a gatepost on a dangerous curve near the Shrewsbury barracks. A stone dislodged from the gatepost then fell on Williams' head, killing him instantly.

13 MAY 1948 Shrewsbury Quarter Sessions were cut short and put on hold until 31 May after the recorder of Shrewsbury, J.F. Bourke, collapsed during the opening.

14 MAY 1839 A sad accident occurred on this day in Market Drayton theatre, where Henry Betty, son of the famous Shrewsbury-born actor William Henry West Betty, was making an appearance as 'Norval' of the play

Douglas, in front of a crowded theatre. During the performance a percussion gun that was being used as a prop by one of the actors was dropped. It went off, exploding only inches from the chest of an actor named John Merrill. The shot killed him instantly, and the subsequent inquest found wadding in the left ventricle of his heart.

15 MAY 1867 Four men died after a cradle chain broke whilst they were descending into the Grange Pits, near Shifnal. An inquiry into their deaths ensued, wherein John Darrell was questioned in order to determine whether his actions led to their demise. Richard Yates, the colliery engineer, was ultimately charged with manslaughter due to the 'lax manner' in which he managed the works: the inquiry discovered that the brass of the fly-wheel had worn away a dangerous amount, meaning that the cog wheel could revolve without locking. The inquest found that the machinery used on the day was not in a 'fit and proper state for use'.

16 MAY 1940 In an act of bravery, Harold Henshaw (23) of Claverley tried – unsuccessfully – to save the life of Hettie Tasker (48), who had fallen 80ft down a well to her death.

17 MAY 1215 On 15 May, King John attempted to persuade Llywelyn the Great, Maelgwyn, Gwenwynwyn and Madog ap Gruffydd to ally themselves with their traditional enemies, John of Monmouth, Hugh Mortimer, Peter fitzhubert and Walter Lacy. Rather than consenting and joining the king's coalition, Llywelyn instead rebelled and allied his troops with the king's enemies. On this day, Llywelyn marched upon Shrewsbury Castle and Shrewsbury town, which were surrendered to him instantly.

18 MAY 1894 On this day Isaac Smith (25), who was a driver by trade, was driving his carriage through the streets of Donnington when the stud chains of his horse became caught on a loose rail that had been left on the road. This rail caused the chain to spring back with some force and strike Smith in the face, breaking both his jaw and collar bone.

In 1215, Llywelyn the Great marched upon Shrewsbury Castle and Shrewsbury town, which were surrendered to him instantly. (Photo by Samantha Lyon)

19 MAY 1871 In 1871, it wasn't particularly unusual to find inexperienced teenagers working in mines. In this instance, a young boy called Ferriday (15) was working as a 'hooker-on' for the Lilleshall Colliery in Wellington. Somehow, in the course of duty, he got his clothes caught on a hook that was making its way back up the pit. This caused the teenager to be dragged part of the way back up. He was almost halfway to the surface before the mistake was rectified. Thankfully the situation was resolved before he suffered a horrible fall.

20 MAY 1900 Two months after he actually passed on, news broke regarding the death of Private Barrett of the King's Shropshire Light Infantry. Barrett died of enteric fever, also known as typhoid fever, which is spread through the lack of adequate hygiene. This disease, when left

untreated, is divided into four stages, with each stage lasting roughly one week. The first week sees the sufferer's temperature rise, and his heartbeat slow; headaches and coughing then set in. During this week there will be a reduction in the number of circulating white blood cells. During the second week, fever soars higher and the patient also suffers from delirium, a characteristic which has lent the disease the nickname of the 'nervous fever'. Pink spots may appear on the upper body, and the abdomen becomes tender and distended. During the third week the sufferer may experience intestinal haemorrhages or perforations in the small intestine. The pain gets worse, and the condition finally kills the sufferer by the end of the fourth week.

21 MAY 1875 On this day Samuel Edwards (46) and William Blackmore (36), both pitmen for the Snailbeach Mining Co., were descending a shaft to do some repair work on the timber of the pit. To do this, both men were placed in a cage suspended on a capstan rope. Before the duo could complete their work, however, the rope gave way at the coupling and the cage fell 150 yards to the bottom of the pit. Both men were killed. During the investigation that followed, it was discovered that the rope was defective, and that one Mr Williams (whose duty it had been to ensure that everything in the pit was in good working order) had failed to notice this obvious deficiency.

22 MAY 1937 After attempting to maul a zoo keeper, a small 4-year-old Himalayan black bear escaped from its cage on a lorry into Albrighton. It was recaptured on this day at Kingsland, 15 miles from where it made its escape. It was seen hiding in a tree, but ran away into the woods before the keepers could arrive. When the keepers eventually caught up with the bear they tried to throw a net over it, but one stumbled – and the bear leapt toward him. At this point, the second keeper ran up behind the bear and struck it over the head with an iron bar, stunning the creature. It was then finally taken to its intended destination, Dudley Zoo. The men were very lucky that they were able to get the better of the animal, as Himalayan black bears are often known to be vicious, as the following quote from *A Book of Man Eaters* explains: 'The Himalayan black bear is a savage animal,

A 4-year-old Himalayan black bear escaped from its cage on a lorry to Albrighton.

sometimes attacking without provocation, and inflicting horrible wounds, attacking generally the head and face with their claws, while using their teeth also on a prostrate victim. It is not uncommon to see men who have been terribly mutilated, some having the scalp torn away from the head.'

23   MAY **1939** Two fatal injuries occurred at Ternhill, Market Drayton, when RAF Corporal Shipp (25) and Corporal John Gowland (37) accidentally crashed into a telegraph pole.

24   MAY **1927** Local media reported on a road accident between Oswestry and Shrewsbury which occurred on the 22 May and injured six people. The accident occurred whilst Harry Morris was driving towards Shrewsbury with his family, including his son and daughter, and crashed

into a car travelling in the same direction. The second car was driven by Charles Collins, with his wife in the passenger's seat. His car was forced into a ditch, and Mrs Collins was thrown out of the car. Morris' car had completely flipped over after crashing into a telegraph pole. Despite a wound to her left shin, Mrs Collins heroically managed to help her husband out of their car, and afterwards made her way over to the Morris family to assist them. Although the whole family suffered various injuries, no one, thankfully, was killed.

25 MAY The grave of the last known sin-eater in the United Kingdom may be found in Ratlinghope churchyard, Shropshire. A 'sin-eater' refers to a person who takes on the sins of a household, during the death of a family member, to absolve their sins and allow them to be at peace. It is known to have been practiced in this county up until the twentieth century and was a ceremony usually performed by a beggar, who would eat bread taken from the chest of the dying person, and drink ale passed to him (or her) over the dying body. A ritual would then be performed in order to transport the sin from the dying soul into the living one. A cynical soul might attest that this was an easy way for a crafty beggar to obtain some free food and drink.

26 MAY 1867 After an absence of seven months, rinderpest revisited John Ravenshaw's farm near Whitchurch, the area where the disease originally made its appearance. The cow, a strong 2-year-old, began to show the symptoms of cattle plague and had to be killed, along with the rest of Ravenshaw's stock, in order to prevent loss and inconvenience to any other farmers in the district.

27 MAY 1773 Following an earthquake on the 26th, a gentleman named John Roberts got up early in the morning on this day and opened his window to see a crack had formed on the ground that was 5in wide. He noticed that the trees were moving despite the fact that there was no wind, and that the River Severn seemed agitated. He ushered his wife and children from the house and ran from his home before the earth began to

convulse. The media later reported that the 30 acres of field were broken up and looked to contain huge chasms, and that twenty large oak trees had fallen into the Severn. Near Buildwas Bridge, the earthquake diverted the Severn from its old channel into a new one. Reverend Fletcher of Madeley describes it as follows:

> Go to the ancient bank of the Severn. You come to it and she is gone! You are in the middle of her old bed ... you stand in the deepest part of the channel and yet you are in a wood! Large oaks spread their branches where bargemen unfurled their sales: you walk to-day on solid ground where fishes yesterday swam in 20ft of water. A rock that formed the bottom of the river, has mounted up as a cork and gained a dry place on the bank, while a travelling grove has planted itself in the waters, and a fugitive river has invaded dry land.

28 MAY 1886 On the 19 October, the notorious James Barnett was brought before the Shropshire Quarter Sessions for a crime he committed against Mr Prowse, a commercial traveller, on this day. Although Barnett was his real name, he was a man of many aliases, including James Buchanan, George Percy, Dr John Vivian, George Gray and George Gulph. It seems that while staying at the Victoria Hotel in Whitchurch, Barnett stole a leather bag that contained English money, in addition to old and valuable Roman coins, from a traveller by the name of James Henry Prouse. At the time of this robbery, he was also wanted in connection to a theft that occurred in Manchester, where John Isaacs was robbed of £425. Having already been sentenced to ten years' penal servitude in 1876, Barnett was given the same sentence after being found guilty of this crime.

29 MAY 1868 Morville church was struck by lightning during a dramatic and violent thunderstorm, receiving substantial damage. The lightning struck the south-west pinnacle of the tower, which broke into pieces. The fragments shot in different directions, and one piece, weighing 20lbs, travelled the whole length of the church and fell through the nave.

30 MAY 1897 In Edgmond, Elsie Grice secretly gave birth on this date, and on 17 July was brought before the court and charged with concealment of birth. The father was called up to the stand and was asked whether he would be willing to marry the girl. As he agreed to do so, she was discharged without punishment.

31 MAY 1905 This day marked the beginning of an inquest into a disastrous fire that broke out in Market Drayton in the early hours of the 30th. When a neighbour discovered that Francis Parker's inn was on fire, they immediately summoned the fire brigade. Unfortunately, the flames spread so quickly that the firemen could not enter the building for some time – the smoke and heat were already too intense. When they were finally able to bring the blaze under control, they found the proprietor lying dead on the landing, along with his two children and their nurse, Maggie Morris (15). The unfortunate victims died due to asphyxia or burns, or a combination of the two. The names of the children were Norman Parker, aged 3 years, and William Stanley Parker, aged only 2 months. The origin of the fire was never discovered.

JUNE

Laura's Tower is a short walk from Shrewsbury
Castle, which is believed to be haunted by
Bloudie Jack. (Photo by Samantha Lyon)

1 JUNE 1925 Lacey Frederick Besant of Shifnal was charged with, and convicted of, the manslaughter of Annie Ecclestone and Florence Ralphs, whose deaths occurred after Besant inadvertently knocked them down in her car on 17 May.

2 JUNE 1934 On this day an outbreak of fire occurred at the Holley Cottages in Rowton. At the time Masie Haywood (4) was sleeping in her bed upstairs. Police Constable Evason attempted to get to her room with a ladder, but the intense smoke drove him back out. On his second attempt he was able to drag the child from the other side of the room with a rake, but unfortunately she was found to be dead when they emerged. In all likelihood it would have been the smoke inhalation that caused poor Masie's death, as approximately 50-80 per cent of fire-related deaths are linked to smoke rather than burns. The inhaled smoke often contains a mixture of particles and gasses, particularly carbon monoxide. This, combined with asphyxiation due to the lack of available oxygen, eventually causes death.

3 JUNE 1947 On this day, the Feathers Hotel at Ludlow, one of the 500 listed buildings in the medieval town, was sold for £30,000. This would be the modern-day equivalent of almost £1 million. It is reputed to be one of the most haunted buildings in England and dates back to 1619, when it was built by Rees Jones, a local attorney. Since it became a hotel in 1863, The Feathers Hotel has been one of the main attractions of the town, due in no small part to its ghostly reputation. Room 211 is supposedly home to a jealous ghost who takes an instant dislike to any female guests. One particular visitor claims to have been woken suddenly and dragged off the bed by her hair. Impressively enough, she managed to calm down and go back to sleep, but was woken up a second time to find herself drenched in cold water. Her partner remained blissfully unaware of the chaos that was going on in the room, and slept peacefully all night, reporting only a pleasant, calming, stroking sensation on his cheek. In addition to this obviously embittered ghost is the apparition of a Victorian gentleman, who has been spotted on different occasions walking a dog through room 232 and into the adjoining room. The hotel's

reputation for paranormal activity isn't new by any stretch. In fact, for a period of about five weeks, from May to June 1869, a bizarre sequence of ghostly happenings caused a hefty crowd to gather around the hotel and attracted a lot of media attention. The situation got so out-of-hand that a number of policeman and detectives were called to the premises to keep the peace. Many visitors complained of a succession of fourteen ringing bells that would keep them up during the night. This prompted surveillance of the bells. They appeared to be normal and stationary when the lights were on, but as soon as the lights were turned off they would start to sound. The cook of the hotel at the time was so disturbed by this that she became ill and resigned. Fortunately for the hotel, however, all the paranormal interest profited the establishment greatly.

4   JUNE 1914   Edward Neville Richards (15) received a silver medal from the Royal Society for the Prevention of Cruelty to Animals on this day. He worked at the Freehold Colliery near Opengate and saved a pony that was in danger of being crushed to death between a door and some moving tubs. Richards intervened and saved the pony, but suffered a broken leg and severe flesh wounds in the process.

5   JUNE 1921   A grey Cornish-granite war memorial was unveiled outside St George's Church in Clun to honour the soldiers who fought for the country in the First World War. The tribute cost £340, and the money was raised through public subscription.

6   JUNE 1944   On D-Day the 2nd Battalion of the King's Shropshire Light Infantry landed on Queen Beach near Hermanvill-sur-Mer. The battalion helped in the capture of Caen. Before the attack on Caen, the town had a population of roughly 60,000. On this day, leaflets were dropped on the city asking the locals to escape to the countryside as the bombing would start in a few hours' time. Despite the warning, only a few hundred civilians left. When the bombing eventually began, it resulted in destruction on a massive scale: the streets were filled with rubble and 800 locals lost their lives.

To the memory of the officers, non-commissioned officers, & men of the line, militia & volunteer battalions of the King's Shropshire Light Infantry, who were killed in action, & died of wounds or disease whilst serving with the 2nd battalion of the King's Shropshire L.I. (85th L.I.) in the Transvaal, Orange River Colony, & Cape Colony, during the campaign in South Africa, 1899–1902. This memorial has been erected by their comrades, officers, non-commissioned officers, & men of the line, militia & volunteer battalions of the King's Shropshire Light Infantry.

In 1944, the Second Battalion of the Shropshire Light Infantry helped in the capture of Caen, where 800 locals lost their lives. (Photo by Samantha Lyon)

7   JUNE 1875   Edwin Purstow (45), a watchman for the South Roman Gravels Colliery, turned up to work on this day more than slightly inebriated. His colleague noticed this and realised that working in such a condition would be risky. Rather than informing someone of his co-worker's condition, which would have likely got the man sacked, he instead went underground and completed the work by himself. When he came back to the surface, he let Purstow know that everything was okay and that he could go home. However, as soon as his fellow watchman left Purstow decided to descend the mine anyway. He was never seen alive again. When his body was found, an investigation concluded that he had slipped from the ladder and had fallen to his death.

8   JUNE 1821   On this day, *The Times* reported, 'One of the most melancholy accidents that ever occurred in Shrewsbury or its vicinity.' Early on the morning of 5 June, part of the southern gable wall of the Shrewsbury Theatre collapsed and fell onto the roof of a neighbouring home. Edward Davies, who lived in the house, was asleep with his wife and two children at the time. The roof fell on top of them and forced them down into the kitchen, where they were buried. Elizabeth, Edward's wife, died instantly on impact. Edward was dead before he could be helped out of the ruins, and his oldest son was only able to open his eyes after being pulled from the debris before dying. Miraculously, the youngest child, a toddler, survived the three-storey fall and was almost unharmed. He was found clinging to his mother, having been protected by two spars that fortunately met over him.

9   JUNE 1645   Sir William Croft (52), a colonel in service to Charles I, bravely led the men of Luston to a battle at Stokesay Castle. The Royalists were defeated, and Croft was killed. His epitaph attests that Croft was an 'eminent example of virtue in his life and of valour in his death'.

More than 200 years later, in 1856, Mr Atherston (50), a deputy with the Furnace No. 13 Colliery, suffocated in a mine due to a heavy odourless and colourless deleterious gas known as carbonic acid gas, sometimes referred to as 'chokedamp' or 'blackdamp' in the mining trade. If the concentration in

Sir William Croft led his men into a battle at Stokesay Castle in 1645, where he was killed. (Tony Grist)

A wood panelling outside Stokesay Castle, where the battle was fought. (Ian Griffiths)

the air is great enough (as little as 4 per cent in the atmosphere is sufficient), it causes almost immediate unconsciousness and suffocation. It was another factor that accounted for a great many deaths in the mining profession.

Throughout history, 9 June seems to have been an unfortunate day for miners in Shropshire. On this day in 1885, Pickering (17), who was a horse driver for the Lilleshall Colliery, was riding to a pit in Wellington when he passed under a roof and some tiles gave way. They landed on his head and killed him.

In 1890, John Bailey (41), a miner for the Snailbeach Colliery was injured whilst he was clearing away some rubble from a previous fall. He unknowingly dislodged a large stone, which fell onto him and a colleague, Samuel Evans (71), breaking a number of their ribs. Bailey was given two weeks off work but, due to the fact that Evans was elderly, the second man was told that it was unlikely he would ever work again, which would have been very bad news for his family.

10   JUNE   1646   Today King Charles I officially sent out the proclamation ordering Royalist strongholds – including Ludlow Castle, the last Royalist stronghold in the county – to surrender: 'the more to evidence the reality of our intentions of establishing a happier and lasting peace, [I] require you, upon honourable considerations, to quit those Townes and Castles, and Forts, entrusted by us to you, and to disband all the forces under your several commands.'

There is another guest in Shropshire who many wish would give up her home: the Magpie House Restaurant of Bridgnorth is said to be haunted by a 'Woman in Black' whose two children were drowned in the cellar when the River Severn flooded. She is sometimes seen floating through the walls of the building, crying and mourning her loss.

11   JUNE   1943   In the Second World War the 1st Battalion of the King's Shropshire Light Infantry aided in 'Operation Corkscrew', which concerned capturing the small Italian island of Pantellaria, which was heavily bombarded from air and sea. More than 14,000 bombs were dropped on the

area, and by the time the first of the commandos landed the Italian Admiral Gina Pavesi had already surrendered, having lost fifty-six of his troops, with a further 116 wounded. The surrender occurred on this day. It was the first time that surrender had been won through bombing. Churchill would later be recorded as saying that the only British casualty in the operation was a man who was bitten by a mule.

12   JUNE   1885   Thomas Parton (65), a taxidermist, lived with his wife, Emma, and son, Harry, in Wellington. Thomas was a bit of an eccentric once he'd had a bit of whisky, and had a habit of shrieking things like 'Murder!' for no discernible reason. On this day, a tragic event occurred when Emma and Harry returned from their travels and Thomas returned from his night at the pub. Later that night, the neighbours heard a cry of 'Murder!' Emma emerged from the house a few minutes later and told her startled neighbours that Thomas was dead. During the murder trial that followed, Emma explained that Parton Snr had fallen down the stairs. This assertion attracted a certain amount of suspicion, as Harry was known to be abusive towards his father on occasion. One coroner concluded that the injuries the deceased had sustained were not *entirely* consistent with a fall down the stairs. However, another disagreed. The case was a dramatic one but, despite some evidence of foul play, it seems that the jury were not convinced beyond a reasonable doubt of the son's guilt. When a verdict of 'not guilty' was read out the spectators in the courtroom applauded loudly, leading the judge to angrily chide the room: 'Silence! Who dares make that noise? This is not a theatre!'

13   JUNE   1897   A horrible railway accident took place on the Cambrian railway line at Welshamton on this day at approximately 10 p.m. The train, which had been returning to Lancashire from mid-Wales, crashed. Thirteen coaches and one engine were completely derailed. One employee and eleven passengers were killed, and a further twenty-five were injured. The enquiry revealed that the train had been running at an excessive speed, especially considering the state of the track, and this recklessness surely caused the accident. The Cambrian railway, however, disputed this and claimed that a Lancashire and Yorkshire railway vehicle at the front of the train was the cause.

14   JUNE   1824   Joseph Jones of St Mary's Parish, Bridgnorth, was walking home with his pet, a 9-month-old puppy, from the Stepping Stones Hill, along a public footpath that took him directly to his house. Robert Herbert, gamekeeper to Thomas Whitmore of Apley, was with three other people when he saw Jones. The gamekeeper, infuriated by the sight of Jones, began to load his gun; the keeper's dog, a Newfoundland terrier, also began to bristle threateningly. As the innocent walker drew near, the keeper threatened to shoot his puppy, despite the fact that man and his companion had been keeping to themselves. Then, without warning, Robert Herbert set his Newfoundland onto the puppy, which was horribly mauled during the dogfight that followed. Jones tried his best to save the dog, but Herbert grabbed him by his collar and threw him to the ground. When Jones, who was quite an elderly man, finally managed to get back on his feet, the wicked keeper threw him down yet again. By this time his puppy was petrified and quivering by a hedge. The stunned Mr Jones managed again to struggle to his feet. He picked up the dog and tried to walk away, but Herbert called out (according to local media), 'Seize him, Jip! Kill him, Jip!' Jip the Newfoundland then sank his teeth into Jones' arm, while Herbert picked the puppy up by his hind legs and slit its throat with a knife he produced from his pocket. Herbert was indicted for assault and Mr Bather, who appeared for the prosecution, described the act as, 'one of the most ferocious, brutal and aggravated that ever was brought before a court of justice'. The vicious gamekeeper was ultimately sentenced to six months in prison with hard labour.

15   JUNE   1919   Major J. Becke, Chief Constable of Shropshire, increased the Shropshire Special Constabulary from approximately 300 to 547, an act he believed necessary due to the 'present circumstances of unrest'. Crime in the rest of the country was on the rise, too, increasing by 5 per cent each year from 1915 to 1930. The most common crimes in these years were theft

and break-ins. This can be attributed to the fact that the war was over and society at large was becoming more affluent, providing a lot of opportunity for potential thieves to indulge in a little larceny.

16   JUNE   1918   Two German prisoners by the names of Bruno Sens and Ernest Joseph Leopold Clasnidzer escaped from the Shrewsbury Internment Camp on this day. They were found and recaptured, on the 19 June, in Tipton.

17   JUNE   1740   Corbet Kynaston was one of six members of parliament who were arrested in September 1715 for being 'engaged in a design to support the intended invasion of the kingdom'. Kynaston died on this day in 1740, and since then Kynaston's ghost has harassed the locals near Coton Hall. In 1788, after deciding that they could not cope with the ghost any longer, the locals asked Revd David Evans to pull some heavenly strings and put an end to it. Evans contacted five other priests and asked them to come to Coton Hall to help with the exorcism. Once there, the six priests prayed for Corbet's soul. The ritual involved extensive candle burning and praying, and they eventually managed to convince Kynaston to enter a glass bottle, which they sealed and threw into a nearby lake. The priests gave the locals a 1,000 year guarantee on the banishment, but shortly after the beginning of the nineteenth century locals began to notice strange happenings again – events which included milk churns, pushed by an invisible hand, beginning to roll, and poolside bushes bursting into blue spectral flames.

18   JUNE   1929   A verdict of accidental death was returned following an inquest at Wellington on the body of John Henry Dorricott (35), a farm worker who was killed after being struck by lightning. Dorricott had taken shelter under an oak tree at the time the lightning struck. If you are outside at the time of a lightning strike, there really is no truly safe place to hide. When lightning hits, it either kills or wounds; lightning has an 80 per cent chance of causing long-term damage. The damage inflicted by the electrical discharge is unlikely to be a burn: the strike is more likely to cause nerve damage. It can also disrupt the body's electrical signals, thereby stopping

the heart or the brain. Sometimes it causes the victim to become temporarily paralysed. In the past, victims have forgotten how to breathe, have lost control of their motor functions, or have suffered severe internal bleeding.

19 JUNE 1898 An unfortunate boating accident occurred at Southsea on this day when five men, two of whom were privates of the Shropshire Regiment, took a boat out on the waters. One of the party fell overboard – and the boat was overturned in an effort to rescue him. Both of the privates drowned.

20 JUNE 1952 Benjamin Isaiah Locke, who had been serving a three-year sentence at Shrewsbury Prison for robbery, escaped while working with a number of other prisoners on a farm at Norton in Hales, about 20 miles from Shrewsbury Prison.

21 JUNE 1952 Donald Neil Simon carried out a brutal double murder on this day on Seymore Road, Slough. On the night in question, a witness heard four gunshots, followed by loud screaming. By the time the witness managed to get down to the street, a young man, apparently dead, was lying next to a woman who seemed very close to death. The people in question were Victor Brades and Eunice Simon. Donald, Eunice's husband, was arrested the following day. The situation, as it came out in court, was that the couple had been living apart after Donald began to drink heavily and assault his wife. Eunice obtained a court order that demanded he keep his distance at all times. Eunice then began to see Victor, and when Donald found out he became enraged. Donald tried to plead insanity at his trial, but this defence did not prove entirely convincing after the jury found out that Donald had told a witness, 'I will kill both of them ... I am under treatment for nerves. I'll plead insanity'. He was quickly found guilty and was hanged at Shrewsbury Prison on 23 October.

22 JUNE 1842 An article appeared in the *Salopian Journal* on this day quoting a report that had been commissioned by the government regarding

the working conditions of women, children and young people in mines. Such persons were often used in mines because the coal seams in the Shropshire Coalfield tended to be too narrow for pit ponies. The report revealed that boys as young as 6 sometimes worked in the pits, and talked of the inhumane 'girdle and chain' that the boys wore to pull coal through the passageways. Children would commonly work for sixteen hours a day for a very little wage. The report, strategically illustrated with women and children at work, provoked a strong reaction and shocked the public, who couldn't believe how badly young children were being treated. It also prompted colliery owners to accept responsibility for how their workers were being treated. Following this report, the Mines and Collieries Bill, supported by Anthony Ashley-Cooper, was rather quickly passed. This legislation made it illegal to use children younger than 10 in mines and also prohibited women from working in mines altogether.

23 JUNE 1644 On this day Sir Thomas Mytton, along with Lord Denbigh, captured Oswestry and defended it against the Royalists, who were attempting to recapture it. Following this, Sir Thomas was made the governor of Oswestry. The town was an important one to all involved, as it was thought of as 'the key which opens the door to Wales'.

24 JUNE 1831 On this day Robert Bales and the other workmen in Robert Hall's employment assembled at a public house in order to receive their wages. As strange as this might seem, this method was the custom with their employer. Hall, however, became very unpopular when he arrived and refused to pay the men, insisting that he had already overpaid them. Despite his increasingly unhappy staff, he stood firm and flatly refused to pay them any more money. The men grew angry and went after Hall, who – seeing the mob's reaction – had rushed upstairs and hidden under a bed. He was grabbed, dragged out and violently beaten up by Bales and a number of other men. Bales was arrested and convicted on 1 August. During his trial, the judge reprimanded Hall for paying his employees in a pub, calling it 'careless and unprofessional'. Incredibly, Hall spoke in Bales'

favour. He even said that he would employ Bales again in the future. Due, in part, to this testimony, the prisoner only received a short imprisonment of two weeks.

25 JUNE 1852 Mary Rogers (28) was arrested on this day for the murder of her newborn son, Edwin, in Wistanstow. The crime had occurred the day before. Rogers had asked her mistress, Mrs Lucas, for leave to look after her newborn baby. Lucas consented. Rogers claimed that she wanted to take the baby to her brother's house; he lived at nearby Church Stretton. She walked there, accompanied by two young women who she was living with at the time. When the women parted ways, she carried on – with her healthy baby – in the direction of where she said her brother lived. This was the last time the baby was seen alive. It was found, drowned, hours later in a pond near Lake Lane. It was then revealed that Rogers had no brother: she had killed the baby and then walked home. During the trial, Rogers was described as an innocent, and seemed somewhat unaware of the true extent of her predicament.

Infanticide occurred all too often in the United Kingdom during the eighteenth and nineteenth centuries. The reason for some of these crimes was the unstable financial situation of the mother. Single mothers often were unable to properly support their newborns, and there were no societal aides at the time to economically assist these families. In addition to the financial strains, the prejudices that unmarried women typically had to endure were often unbearable for the women involved.

26 JUNE 1894 Reverend Lord Forester of Willey died on the 22 June after an illness that was brought on by a chill. He had been suffering for nearly a month, and the media regularly reported on his health to the concerned public. His funeral took place on this day at Willey Park, Broseley.

27 JUNE 1939 On this day Charles Wells received a horrible shock when he discovered the bodies of Mrs Venables and William Bufton. Bufton was missing the better half of his head, which looked as though it had been

blown off with a shotgun. Venables had a huge wound in her chest, a wound which was so deep that it exposed the organs beneath. The list of suspects was almost non-existent, as the two were very well-liked and had no enemies to speak of. An investigation revealed the only suspect to be George Owen, a man who was related to Bufton through marriage and who had been admitted to Shrewsbury Hospital after trying to cut out his own throat. As it transpired, the latter injury was not life-threatening and was seen as simply a 'cry for help'. Owen, as it was revealed in court, had threatened Bufton not long before his death. His threat came about after an argument in which Owen accused Bufton of being 'nothing but an idle parasite', who 'wasted all his time' at Rhos cottage with Venables. The man believed that Venables was having an affair with Bufton. He was arrested for the double murder, but by this point his mental health had deteriorated: he barely had a grasp on reality. He was brought before the Shrewsbury Assizes but was deemed unfit to plead due to his mental state.

28 JUNE 1963 Kenneth Raymond Cooper (32) died under tons of rubble, along with four others, on this day. Tragic as this was, his last act was to save the lives of his workmates. He was working in the cellars of a demolition site in the centre of Shrewsbury when he noticed the floor above him was close to caving in. He didn't have time to escape himself, but he shouted for his colleagues, who were working above, to run and get to safety.

29 JUNE 2008 On this day, the prison service revealed that Donald Neilson, also known as 'The Black Panther', was suffering from the progressive and ultimately fatal Amyotrophic Lateral Sclerosis (ALS), more commonly known as Motor Neuron Disease. This disease makes the sufferer weak and causes muscle spasms, difficultly speaking, swallowing and, eventually, breathing. Neilson was pronounced dead in prison on 18 December 2011, after a thirty-five-year stay.

Neilson rose to infamy through a series of robberies, murders and a high-profile kidnapping. He was born on 1 August 1936. Between 1971–75, Neilson shot and killed five people before being arrested on 11 December 1975. He was sentenced to life in prison in July the following year.

Neilson began his career in crime when his business began to fail financially. In a desperate bid to keep afloat, he became Britain's most wanted man. Most of his victims were postmasters, but one was a young heiress whom he targeted after reading an article in the *Daily Express* that revealed she had inherited £82,500 from her father. The girl in question was 17-year-old sixth-form student, Lesley Whittle from Highley. Neilson kidnapped Whittle from her Shropshire home on 14 January 1975 and demanded a large ransom from her family. The kidnap ended in tragedy when Whittle's body was found in a shaft, naked and hanging from a wire cable, her feet inches from the ground. The post-mortem examination indicated she had likely died forty-eight hours after her capture.

Neilson was caught by police officers Tony White and Stuart Mackenzie, who stopped him on the A60 when they noticed him walking past them carrying a holdall and looking nervous in the presence of their police car.

30 JUNE 1882 Joseph Kynaston was killed while working in a mine at the Ifton colliery after being hit on the head by 'a fall of roof'. There was no certified manager on the site and unfortunately no one had been left in charge at the pit. At Oswestry police court on 13 July, George Edwin Hill-Trevor and John Williams were charged with manslaughter. The case was dismissed, as it could not be proved that they were directly responsible for Kynaston's death.

This once again seems to be an unfortunate day for miners in Shropshire as, on this same date in 1911, poor Thomas Bate (71), who was working as a labourer for the Woodhouse Colliery, was descending from a timber truck that he was unloading when he slipped and fractured his thigh. This accelerated his pre-existing heart disease, meaning that he became very sick for a number of months and eventually died on the 6 February 1912.

JULY

The graveyard located in Shrewsbury Abbey, which
was rebuilt on the site of an old Saxon church.
(Photo by Samantha Lyon)

1   JULY **1899**   William Knight (57), a sinker for the Wombridge Station Colliery, was working on this day and was instructed to reopen an old shaft. After doing so, he almost instantly collapsed and then perished. The cause of death was found to be suffocation due to chokedamp, a gas that is very often found when a coal mine is poorly ventilated or abandoned, such as this one was. Chokedamp happens because the coal is exposed to oxygen, which it absorbs, expelling carbon dioxide and water vapour as a reaction to this. Another factor that would have encouraged the chokedamp would have been the time of year: in July, the likelihood of hotter weather is increased, which causes the coal to produce even more carbon dioxide. Thousands of lives would have been saved in the eighteenth and nineteenth centuries had they the electronic gas detectors that miners make use of today.

When William Knight opened an old shaft, he collapsed and died instantly due to 'choke damp'.

2   JULY **1938**   David Eiron Llewelyn, a teacher at Ludlow Grammar School, was sentenced on this day at the Shrewsbury Assizes. The teacher, in a movement of insanity, attacked and wounded his wife. He then tried to take his own life, an act that was still a crime at this point. He was found guilty but insane. He was therefore detained at His Majesty's pleasure.

3   JULY **1857**   On this day, a tragic accident took place during a festival that *The Times* described as 'M. Jullien's annual musical fête in conjunction with the Shropshire Horticultural Society's show.' The event occurred on a makeshift island that had been temporarily constructed on the

Severn specifically for the occasion, referred to as 'the Island of Poplars'. It is estimated that, over the course of the day, 10,000 people visited the island, the majority of them women and children. Shortly after 10 p.m. the entertainment drew to a close with a dazzling firework display. As soon as the last firework was released, the visitors began to make their way home, using a bridge of boats to get to shore. Unfortunately, due to the actions of a few merrily intoxicated partygoers, the temporary bridge began to sway, swinging heavily from one side to the other. This eventually caused the punt which was the central portion of the bridge to capsize. Although some were able to escape and scramble to shore, many others were trapped beneath the punt. The survivors were left in a poor state: some had nearly drowned, some were badly cut and some sported broken bones. It took a whole twenty minutes to reach the people who were trapped under the punt: they drowned before anyone could get them out. Among the deceased

In 1857, a makeshift island was placed on the River Severn for a festival, following which an accident occurred and many Salopians lost their lives. (Photo by Samantha Lyon)

were Edward Joseph Ditcher (2), John Price (11), and his sister Ann (14). At least ten people drowned. However, exactly how many people died in the accident is unknown, since a lot of bodies were swept away by the Severn and never found.

4   JULY 1811 The Ludlow Meeting in Shropshire, reported upon by the *Sporting Magazine*, began with an excellent race by Mr Keen's 3-year-old. However, tragedy struck the stables the next day when his mare, Parvula, an 8 stone 5lbs 5-year-old, 'ran against a man who was endeavouring to cross the Course, and in consequence was thrown down, by which accident her near leg was broken, and her rider (R. Spencer), was most dreadfully cut and hurt about the head and face. It was thought that Parvula would have won easy.'

5   JULY 1944 After the death of their parents, Dennis O'Neill (12) and his two younger brothers were committed to the care of Newport County Borough Council. It was on this day that Dennis and his brother Terrence had the unfortunate luck of being placed in the care of Reginald (31) and Esther Gough (29) from Bank Farm near Minsterley. They were separated from their younger brother, Frederick (7), who was sent to a home nearby. The Gough's contract required that they treat the children as their own, and specified that in return they should receive £1 a week. On the 9 January of the following year, Esther Gough made a call to Dr Holloway Davies to tell him that Dennis was having a fit. The doctor arrived a few hours later to find him already dead. It was later discovered that Dennis had already been dead for about six hours – long before the doctor received the phone call. Following an inquest, it was discovered that Dennis had suffered cardiac failure following a heavy beating to the chest. It was also established that he had been repeatedly struck on the back with a stick. On top of all of this, both Dennis and his brother were severely underweight, with septic ulcers on their feet. Mr H.H. Maddocks, for the prosecution, spoke about Dennis' condition, saying that he was, 'undernourished and practically starved. No fat was found on him.' He also gave evidence in the form of photographs

that showed how badly his back and chest had been beaten. Apparently this was not a one-off beating, either. The boys would often be violently struck after they tried to 'steal' food from the pantry. Richard Gough was charged with manslaughter on 3 February. The judge originally instructed the jury that Esther could not be found guilty of manslaughter as she did not possess the strength necessary to inflict the wounds that had caused Dennis' death. However, she could still be found guilty of neglect and wilful ill-treatment. This view soon changed, however, and Esther was also charged with manslaughter on the 12th. On 19 March, the jury took twenty minutes to find Richard Gough guilty of manslaughter. He received six years in prison; Esther was sentenced to six months' imprisonment. The details of this case went on to inspire Agatha Christie's play *The Mousetrap*.

6   JULY 1844   In January of this year a serious burglary took place in Shropshire. Constable Jeremiah Smith was the man responsible for carrying out the enquiries. He soon identified Richard Freeman of Upton Magna as a suspect and obtained a warrant to search his property. Smith and Benjamin Burgwin, the victim of the burglary, went together to Freeman's home to carry out a search of his house – a search which, they hoped, would locate the stolen goods. Once they arrived, Smith arrested Freeman on suspicion of burglary. Freeman became incensed and struck out at Smith, who attempted to calm him. After a brief scuffle, Freeman, seemingly mollified, invited Smith into his house to conduct the search. As soon as Smith entered, however, Freeman picked up an axe that was propped up near the doorway. He lashed out wildly with it as Smith gripped his collar and attempted to restrain him. After several attempts to hit him, the axe caught Smith on the head and he collapsed, unconscious, to the floor. Freeman was about to cause more injury when Burgwin entered, carrying a stick, which he waved threateningly at Freeman. The burglar took this opportunity to attempt an escape. Freeman was eventually found and taken to court. He received a sentence of twenty years' transportation. He was one of the 224 convicts on the HMS *Agincourt*, which departed on this day.

7   JULY 1866   While clearing the site for the new Shrewsbury railway station, which was once the remains of the old abbey, the workers uncovered a collection of thirty or forty human skeletons. The abbey was founded in approximately 1100, but was built on the site of an older Saxon church. It was said that the teeth were amazingly well-preserved, and that aside from one skull with a deep dent in it, it appeared that none of the skeletons had died due to injuries. Curiously, no remains of clothing or coffins could be seen, despite the fact that the bodies seemed to have been laid down with care, rather than carelessly thrown into the ground.

The remains of human skeletons were discovered under the old abbey in 1866. (Photo by Samantha Lyon)

8   JULY 1952   Harry Huxley (43) was hanged at Shrewsbury Prison for the murder of his girlfriend, Ada Royce (32), following a trial at Ruthin Assizes on 20 May. Although attempts were made to secure a reprieve for Huxley, the Home Secretary believed that there were insufficient grounds to cause him to interfere with the sentencing of the crime.

9   JULY 1646   On this day the Royalist garrison of Ludlow Castle, having received the proclamation of the month before, surrendered to Parliamentarian Commander Sir William Brereton. By this date, as the First Civil War (1642–46) drew to a close, a number of other Shropshire castles had been captured by the Parliamentarians. Bridgnorth Castle and Ludlow Castle held out the longest, with Bridgnorth being taken in April. During the four-year conflict, thousands of people lost their lives. It is impossible, however, to know the actual figure as there was often confusion regarding whether people died due to disease or as a result of wounds. Unreliable as such figures might be, a conservative estimate for war-related disease would be approximately 100,000 people. Historians estimate that a further 84,830 died from war-related violence.

10   JULY 1908   Frederick Wale (44), the vicar of Holy Trinity, Shrewsbury, fell to his death in the Pleiades while staying at Blonay. He was on his way to see the view of Lake Geneva and Mont Blanc from the mountain. When he did not return, a search party was sent out and his mutilated body was found at the foot of the Rochers de Naye, a mountain nearly 7,000ft high. It seems that vicar was in bad health and had taken a trip to Switzerland in order to speed up his recovery.

11   JULY 1887   *The Times* reported on a fatal accident that had occurred on the 8th when William Saunders, who was employed as a constable at the Earl of Shrewsbury's Brereton Collieries, was unintentionally killed by fellow Police Constable O'Leary of the Staffordshire Constabulary. On the day in question, O'Leary was at the house of local gamekeeper, Henry Littler. Not long after his arrival, Saunders appeared at the scene, accompanied by

a fellow police officer. At that point, O'Leary picked up a gun that he found leaning near a railing of the house and, in jest, aimed it at the two men. One of the police officers, it was later reported, joked with O'Leary that he had no business handling the gun as he had no licence. Unaware that the gun was loaded, O'Leary pulled the trigger – and the gun went off. Saunders was hit. Although efforts were instantly made to obtain medical assistance, the injury was severe and Saunders died shortly after receiving the wound. He left behind a grieving wife and six children.

12   JULY **1902**   A terrible pit accident took place at the 'Stafford' Collieries of the Lilleshall Co. William George Cartwright, Daniel Williams and William Pickering had been hired to repair a valve in the pit. After the repairs were done, the men began their ascent to the surface. Suddenly, the beam they were standing on gave way, causing Cartwright and Pickering to fall. When they recovered Cartwright's body from the bottom of the pit it was found to be horribly mangled, but Pickering was fortunate enough to avoid hitting the sides of the pit. He was found clinging to a rod to prevent himself from drowning in the deep water. Williams was the most fortunate of all, as the part of the beam he was standing on had not fully collapsed, meaning that he was able to shout for help and was brought quickly to the surface.

13   JULY **1833**   On this day, John Causer died of stab wounds inflicted by George Hayward (20). The two men, both from Beckbury, had been engaged in an intense argument concerning Causer's sister, who could not seem to get the message across to Hayward that she was not interested in pursuing a romantic relationship. Causer warned Hayward to keep his distance and to leave his sister alone. In response to this, an inebriated Hayward went home, retrieved a knife, and returned to stab Causer twice in the stomach. These stab wounds caused so much damage that the wounded man's intestines protruded. He suffered a prolonged and painful death over nearly five days. Hayward stood trial on 2 August. At his trial, the judge explained to the jury that if they believed the accused had acted in the heat of the moment,

it would mitigate the charge to that of manslaughter. The jury, in rejecting this possibility, must have come to the conclusion that a walk to and from his home (in order to collect the murder weapon) would have given the prisoner sufficient time to regain his composure and he was convicted of the murder. He was hanged there a few days later, on 5 August.

14 JULY 1954 On this day it was announced that the remains of Tong Castle, near Shifnal, were to be demolished by a Territorial Army unit as a part of their training.

The original castle was built in the twelfth century and has since been described as an 'architectural mongrel'. During the Civil War, the castle was defended by William Carlis, who is also known to have offered Charles II sanctuary in the famous oak near his home at Boscobel. The original castle was demolished in 1765, and in 1911 the house built in its stead was badly damaged by fire. The site that the castle once rested on is now part of the M54 motorway.

Tong Castle was defended by William Carlis, who once offered Charles II sanctuary in a large oak tree. (THP)

15 JULY 1694 Thomas Gilbert of Rowton, who was known as 'the Bishop of Shropshire' at the time, was an ejected minister following the Act of Uniformity of 1662, or Black Bartholomew's Day. This was a movement which cast out any minister that refused to adhere to the Book of Common Prayer. He was once referred to as 'the common epitaph-maker for

dissenters'. Gillbert (76) suffered from extreme poverty in his final years and died on this day before being buried in the chancel of St Aldate's.

16 JULY **1914** Quarryman Thomas Henry Davies (55) was working in the Ruckley Quarry on this date, on a ledge 8ft off the ground. He was working away at the sandstone with his pick when a sizable chunk of sandstone fell from the quarry above him. It managed to land on him in such a way as to cause a fracture of his left leg as well as other internal injuries. Despite everyone's best efforts, the injuries were found to be too severe to survive and Davies passed away.

17 JULY **1453** John Talbot, the 1st Earl of Shrewsbury, was born in 1384 in Blakemere and was killed on this day at the Battle of Castillon near Bordeaux. His embalmed heart was subsequently buried under the doorway of St Alkmund's Church, Whitchurch. Talbot, who was

John Talbot, the 1st Earl of Shrewsbury, had his heart embalmed under the doorway of St Alkmund's Church, Whitchurch. (THP)

mentioned in William Shakespeare's historic play *Henry VI, Part 1*, is generally portrayed and remembered as a great soldier. However, his reputation isn't always glowing, and some historians have raised doubts over his leadership. Brave as he was, he was considered a bit too rash, too eager to begin battles with reluctant opponents. For example, in 1429, when he suffered a famous defeat at Patay, Talbot was advised by Sir John Fastolf not to fight. Talbot decided to go ahead with the battle anyway. The French were spurred on by Joan of Arc, and they fought with such spirit that they destroyed the English. Historically this was fairly unusual, and Fastolf's side suffered greatly. Most of the English army was killed or captured. Fastolf managed to escape, with a few others, and the French suffered only very minimal losses.

18 JULY 1898 *The Times* reported a tragic murder that had taken place in Much Wenlock the day before. The grim discovery was made by Francis Josiah Danks, a school teacher, who heard a noise from outside his house and went out to investigate. He found Mrs Lawley and her daughter, both in their nightgowns and covered in blood. The source of the bleeding was later discovered to be a large cut across Mrs Lawley's throat. Despite her horrendous injury, she was still desperately clinging to life, and Danks contacted the police and doctors immediately. By the time Dr Mackenzie reached the scene, however, Mrs Lawley was dead and the daughter was distraught with grief. The perpetrator was later discovered to be the victim's husband, William Lawley, who had been recently released from a private lunatic asylum after a nine-month visit. Despite his release, he was still meant to be in the company of an attendant at all times. Instead, he managed to escape, catch a train to Shrewsbury, and walk 12 miles to his old home to commit the deed. The police constable who came to the scene discovered Lawley as he left his home, via the back door, where he was arrested.

19 JULY 1892 Richard Bromley was tried in Shrewsbury before Mr Justice Cave for the wilful murder of his infant, William Henry Bromley, on the 7 April at Llanyblodwell. Bromley had lived near Oswestry with his

wife and children, and seemed completely happy until six months before the crime, when he began to drink far too much. On 4 April, a big argument led to his wife leaving their home, with their three children, for a stay at her stepfather's house. On the following Wednesday, an inebriated Bromley arrived at her temporary home late in the evening to convince his family to return, and was successful in doing so. The next morning Mrs Bromley had to leave for Oswestry on business, and so left her sleeping husband in charge of the children. When he woke up, however, he assumed that his wife had left him again. Infuriated, he stalked downstairs and found a razor; he then cut the throats of all of his children, told a neighbour what he had done, and then attempted to take his own life. The neighbour, Sir John Fastalf, immediately contacted the police and obtained medical assistance, saving the lives of all but the youngest child. After his recovery, Bromley was examined by Dr Strange, the superintendent of the Shropshire and Montgomery Lunatic Asylum. Dr Strange claimed that the prisoner had likely been suffering from 'transitory mania' at the time of the offence. Evidence also proved a family history of insanity, as well as indications that he had suffered bouts of insanity previously. He was deemed guilty but insane, and detained at His Majesty's pleasure.

20 JULY 1581 Sir George Blount of Kinlet was a firm supporter of the Protestant Reformation, and extremely loyal to King Henry VIII, who had introduced various religious changes. Despite his continued loyalty to the crown, his religious views changed over time, and he gradually became just as loyal and zealous about his newly discovered Roman Catholic faith. It seems that he was both passionate and unrelenting in his new-found loyalty. He threw his wife out in the 1570s and disinherited his daughter, Dorothy, after she angered him by becoming involved with his page, John Purslow. In his will he favoured his nephew, Roland Lacon, a man whose

beliefs were as firmly Roman Catholic. Blount died on this day at the age of 67. In Kinlet church there is an alabaster monument to Blount and his wife, Constance Talbot. In the monument they are depicted kneeling with their children, John (who died young) and Dorothy. This statue is much admired by students of sepulchral architecture.

Not long after Blount's death, Dorothy got married to the page, despite Blount begging her not to on his deathbed. It wasn't long after this that, according to legend, his soul came back to terrorise his village. He was infuriated that his daughter would disobey him. On one occasion, when the happy family were sitting down for dinner, his ghost appeared with a horse and carriage: the ghostly Blount then drove the carriage along the dining table, nearly scaring an old servant to death. After that, his ghost was seen often, riding a black horse and angrily terrorising the village. In an attempt to purge the house of his spirit, his descendant's tore down the old hall and built a new one further from the church. This did nothing, however, to discourage Blount, who continued to harass the locals, riding his spectral horse on the road and throwing anyone aside who tried to get in his way. According to legend, clergymen finally contained his spirit in what has been described as a 6in long bottle, filled three parts with a dark liquid. It was said that if it were ever reopened, 'Old Blount' would be free again to haunt Kinlet. The bottle was put in Blount's tomb in Kinlet church, where it remained until the early twentieth century – when a brave and curious historian finally opened it. The solution inside was investigated and it turned out to be photographic developer.

27   JULY 1403 The Battle of Shrewsbury was fought on this day, and is believed to have taken place in Battlefield, just 3 miles north of Shrewsbury. This famous battle was made mention of in William Shakespeare's historical play *Henry IV, Part 1*. King Henry IV led an army against the rebel forces of Henry 'Harry Hotspur' Percy who planned to defeat the king and divide England with his co-conspirators Edward Mortimer and Glyn Dwr. Although neither side seemed particularly eager to engage, negotiations between them failed and the fight began shortly before dusk. The battle was the first one

where English archers fought one another in England, and demonstrated just how deadly the longbow is. During the hand-to-hand combat which followed, Harry Hotspur was killed. The fighting ended, within two hours, shortly after Hotspur's death was noticed. He was reportedly killed when he opened his visor and received an arrow in the face. After Hotspur's death, his nephew Thomas Nevill buried him in Whitchurch. However, after rumours started spreading that Harry Hotspur had cheated death and was still alive, the king demanded that his body be dug up. His remains were then salted and put on display in Shrewsbury, impaled on a spear in the marketplace.

At the battle of Shrewsbury, Henry Hotspur was killed when he opened his visor and received an arrow to the face. (THP)

As if this wasn't proof enough of Hotspur's demise, his head was then sent to York and impaled on the north gate. His remains were finally returned to his widow, Elizabeth, months later.

The king's forces lost 3,000 men during the battle, and the rebel forces lost 2,000, despite beginning the battle with fewer men. Years later, in 1409, a chapel was erected in Battlefield to commemorate the soldiers that died on both sides.

22 JULY 1884 On this day, in the village of Highley, John Price, a local labourer, went into a pub with a loaded gun. He went to the bar and threatened the landlady, who did her best to keep her calm. She told him to put it away and leave, but instead he turned to a man named Thomas Greenwood – and a blast sounded. The shot lodged in Greenwood, who died instantly.

23 JULY 1886 On this day, a local surgeon dentist by the name of George William was sentenced to two months in prison with hard labour. He had been tried and convicted for beating his wife. During the trial it came to light that George often mistreated his wife and denied her money to buy necessities such as clothes and food. On this particular occasion George brutally beat his wife with a dog whip, inflicting large cuts across her back and shoulders. Following the announcement of the guilty verdict, the crowd in the courtroom applauded loudly.

24 JULY 1883 Matthew Webb of Dawley became the first recorded person to swim the length of the English Channel independent of artificial aids. Webb tragically passed away during his final stunt, which involved a hazardous swim through the Whirlpool Rapids of Niagara River, below Niagara Falls. Webb arrived in America, with his family, determined to perform a stunt which many warned him was both dangerous and suicidal. At approximately 4.30 p.m. he jumped off his boat and was caught instantly by a big wave, which lifted him up and then dragged him under. He eventually reappeared, but was promptly dragged 40m under again by a

whirlpool. This was the last time Webb was seen alive. His body was eventually collected four days later, along with two Native Americans who had also been in the water. Webb's body was sporting a long gash across the head, originally sparking the belief that, when he was dragged under, he had hit his head on a rock and become knocked unconscious, causing him to drown. An autopsy discovered that neither drowning nor the blow to the head – which had fractured his skull – was the cause of his death. Instead, the cause was found to have been the massive weight the water imposed on him when he was dragged under, which had paralysed his nerve centres and prevented him from being able to breathe or use his arms or legs. He was buried in Oakwood Cemetery, near Niagara.

Matthew Webb drowned when his nerve centres were paralysed, meaning that he was unable to use his arms or legs underwater. (THP)

25 JULY 1403 Thomas Percy, who achieved the title of knight banneret during his time, was born in Shrewsbury and was defeated, captured and killed during the Battle of Shrewsbury. He was buried on 23 July in Whitchurch, but was dug up again on this day, had his head cut off and put on display on one of the gates of York. His body was exhibited in Shrewsbury.

26 JULY 1948 General Sir Bernard Paget unveiled a war memorial at Shrewsbury School on this day. The memorial is a marble wall that circles halfway around a statue of Sir Philip Sidney, the famous poet and soldier. The encompassing wall displays the name of every former pupil of Shrewsbury School who has died for their country.

27   JULY 1954   Mr J. Coles, his wife and his two children were residents of Bridgnorth when, following a visit to Mâcon in southern France, they were admitted to hospital after their car was overturned. The accident was believed to have been caused by a burst tyre.

28   JULY 1857   On this day *The Times* reported on the sentencing of Henry Humphreys, who had been found guilty of stabbing and wounding Emma Cryle with intent to cause grievous bodily harm. The incident occurred on 10 January at Ludlow, when Cryle decided to go a pub called the Spread Eagle. While there, she saw the prisoner and a few other men talking, and left fifteen minutes later. She was followed not long after by Humphreys, who walked with her for a short time. After a brief conversation, it was agreed that, in exchange for a shilling, Cryle would do something – exactly what, I leave with the reader – for him. She demanded the shilling up front, but when Humphreys refused these terms she decided against the exchange and began to walk away. He then grabbed her, stabbed her three or four times in the groin, kicked her in the back, and left her in the street to die. Her wounds were so severe that she lost her sight for a time, and it took several hours to stem the bleeding. Fortunately, however, Cryle survived, although it took her a month to fully recover.

29   JULY 1825   John Morris was brought before Justice Burbrough for the manslaughter of William Richards (19). The two had arranged an illegal 'pitched battle'. A pitched battle is when two parties agree on a time and place to fight. The fight went on unimpeded, but there were complications afterwards when Richards went home and became extremely ill. His mother claimed that, when he returned home, he had a huge swelling under his throat. She therefore demanded that he go to bed. Later on, Richard experienced a series of fits that lasted until 3 a.m. the following morning. He died soon afterwards.

30   JULY 1827   This was a time of severe thunderstorms throughout England. In Shrewsbury three cottages, all of which housed blind men, were struck by lightning. The cottages instantly went up in flames, but the three blind inhabitants miraculously escaped without a single injury.

31 JULY 1910 Almer Turley, an ironworker employed at Oakengate, seemingly experienced a bout of temporary insanity and brutally attacked his wife on this day. At the time Mrs Turley was carrying their 3 month-old-baby, but this didn't stop Turley from severing her jugular vein with his razor. Mrs Turley tried to escape, but fell dead on the doorstep of a nearby cottage as she attempted to get help. Afterwards Turley cut his own throat with the same razor. As a final gruesome note, the local media reported that he almost severed his head from his body as he did so.

AUGUST

The Severn and Kingsland, Shrewsbury. (Library of Congress, LC-ppmsc-08838)

1 **AUGUST 1823** Local media reported on a case in which Edmund Whitcombe, who had been a local surgeon and coroner for Shrewsbury, was accused of misconduct. While investigating the murder of Sarah Newton he met with the prime suspect, Mr Newton, and agreed to argue his innocence in return for monetary gain. Unfortunately for Whitcombe, another surgeon, by the name of Coley, was also involved in the case and prevented Whitcombe's attempt to pervert the course of justice. Coley disagreed with the conclusions Whitcombe drew, and put forth the view that the numerous lacerations which had caused Sarah Newton's death were likely to have been suffered during a beating. Whitcombe dismissed this theory and tried to convince the jury that Sarah's death had arisen from a haemorrhage and that it occurred naturally and could not feasibly have been propagated by violence. He also convinced the jury that it was not necessary to view the body – knowing that there were various bruises and cuts that would have swayed their conclusions in a direction that would not benefit him. It was later revealed that Whitcombe had never interviewed the vital witness, George Edwards, who had seen Sarah Newton shortly before her death and could verify that she was in good health. Whitcombe was forced out of his position as county coroner for Shropshire on this date.

2 **AUGUST 1923** During a particularly vicious gale, an old elm tree in the quarry was blown down and landed on a young girl by the name of Marjorie Adams (6). She was killed by the fall.

3 **AUGUST 1937** While in the act of chasing down three boys who had escaped from the local youth centre, Constable Henry Speake (21) was forced into the freezing cold Severn. The temperature of the water was so drastically low that it caused Speake to suffer a fatal heart attack. What Speake suffered from is a physiological response known as 'the cold shock response'. This happens often when people fall through thin ice and into freezing cold water. Researchers from the *British Medical Journal* say that even a small drop in temperature can lead to an increase in the number of people who suffer a heart attack. This is why most people have heart

attacks during the winter months. Such cold temperatures affect the heart as it increases blood pressure and the probability of blood clots. Sudden submersion in cold water while the weather is hot (as the weather may have been in August) has often been known to cause heart attacks even in young and healthy people. This may have happened on this occasion, as no time was allowed for Speake's body to acclimatise and his sudden immersion would have caused arrhythmic heart beats and hyperventilation, putting too much strain on the cardiac system.

4 **AUGUST** 1828 Sergeant John Horton decided on 31 March, while he was having a drink at The Whimsey Inn, that it was about time he confronted the notorious William Stevenson (31). Stevenson was most commonly known by his alias 'Billy Sugar', and was a collier from Churchbridge with a ferocious reputation. Locals knew that he was in the habit of carrying a knife around with him in case a police officer attempted to make an arrest. At the time warrants were out against Stevenson, who had worked his way into significant debt. Sergeant Horton approached Stevenson and told him that he was under arrest. Stevenson responded by saying that he was on his way home from work and would be very grateful if Horton would allow him time to go home and wash before being taken in. Horton permitted this – but when Stevenson finally returned, he was carrying a large knife. He proceeded to stab Horton, who died soon afterwards of the wound. Stevenson was tried for the murder and received a guilty verdict at the Shropshire Assizes. This day marks his execution, which was attended by 5,000 onlookers. Rather than looking terrified or repentant, Stevenson was said to have had a look of 'eager curiosity' at facing the

When William Stevenson met the noose he was said to have had a look of 'eager curiosity'.

gallows, and even helped the hangman with placing the noose around his neck. His body was afterward passed along to the Royal Salop Infirmary for dissection. He was buried behind St Mary's Church.

5   **AUGUST** 1642   The Battle of Maserfield, often referred to as Cogwy by the Welsh, was fought on this day in the town now known as Oswestry. The battle saw a conflict between the Anglo-Saxon Kings Penda of Mercia, who was a pagan, and Oswald of Northumbria, a Christian. The extent of the casualties is unknown, but the battle was a Mercian victory, resulting in the death of Oswald. As he was a Christian, Oswald was revered as a saint after his grisly death, which involved rather a lot of dismemberment. Pieces of his body were distributed around the battlefield as trophies, and his head and arms were mounted on poles. It is said that in the year following the war, Oswiu, Oswald's brother, returned to the site and retrieved Oswald's remains. It is due to King Oswald's dramatic demise that the town is said to have received its name, 'Oswald's Tree'.

6   **AUGUST** 1958   On this day the local media reported on a trial which was set to take place on 14 August. The case involved three young prisoners who had attempted to escape Shrewsbury Prison on 24 July. On the day in question, the prisoners tied up one prison officer and viciously beat another on the head, causing a massive gash to open up on his forehead. The escape was unsuccessful.

7   **AUGUST** 1887   The Kynastons, who lived at Fenemore Bank, Baschurch, were not a content family. The couple had five children and Charles Kynaston, the husband, was having an illicit affair with a servant named Emma Brayne, who eventually fell pregnant. His wife, Betsy, had a serious drinking problem. They were sleeping in separate rooms – and if they spoke, it was only to argue. The servants had witnessed many an argument and a beating: Charles had even thrown his wife out of the house on more than one occasion. Charles claimed that on this day he had been woken by a loud bang. He quickly jumped out of bed and went to his wife's

room, only to find her lying dead in her bed. At first, his story was believed and the death was believed to have been the result of suicide. However, when the police and surgeons analysed the angle of the gunshot wound, they realised that suicide would not have been possible. The police then looked to Charles. However, despite the disharmony of his marriage, there was inadequate evidence to charge him with the murder, and as such he was acquitted.

8   AUGUST   1829   Robert Poupelt was indicted for the manslaughter of Richard Evans. The death was generally believed to have been a result of extreme provocation – the deceased appeared to have been looking for a fight. On the night he died, Evans hit Poupelt on the head. Rather than immediately retaliating, Poupelt kept his calm and warned him never to do it again. His words weren't much of a deterrent to Evans, however, and a brawl broke out. Eventually, a few of Evans' friends dragged him away. When they were relatively convinced that Evans had cooled off they released him – whereupon he promptly took a running jump at Poupelt, and the fight continued. It was to be the last thing he ever did – Poupelt struck back, and the attacker dropped. Medical evidence later revealed that Evans had broken his neck when he landed, as he was 'in the habit of falling when he received a blow'. The autopsy also revealed inflamed intestines and bruises on the left and right temple. Poupelt was found guilty of manslaughter, but he was discharged, and the only punishment he received was that of a fine.

In criminal law, provocation was a genuine legal defence but was only available against murder. By using a defence of provocation, a charge of murder could be reduced to involuntary manslaughter. It was employed when a solicitor could argue that the defendant experienced a temporary but total loss of control in response to someone else's provocative behaviour. This differs from insanity, which involves more of a permanent loss of control. First developed in the English legal system in the sixteenth and seventeenth centuries, provocation allowed the court to consider the *mens rea* ('guilty mind'), i.e. the intentions of the defendant. If they had indeed lost control for a brief moment, then they did not intend to commit murder and so shouldn't be tried for that crime. The defence was eventually abolished on 4 October 2010 with the Coroners and Justice Act (2009).

9 AUGUST 1788 This day saw the execution of John Pyheroe (36), who hanged at the gallows at Old Heath for the murder of his wife.

10 AUGUST 1651 Fifteen years before the Great Fire of London, a major fire erupted in Market Drayton, which destroyed 70 per cent of the town. It is known as 'the Great Fire of Market Drayton' and took place on this day. It was believed to have started at a bakery and spread quickly through the town due to the half-timbered buildings with their thatched roofs. To this day a bell exists in the centre of town, ready for people to ring if ever they witness the beginnings of another destructive fire. Charles II ordered a collection to help Market Drayton recover.

Charles II. (Library of Congress, LC-US262-38492)

11 AUGUST 1830 On this day, *The Times* reported that Hannah Harley (19) had been indicted on two counts of attempted murder by arsenic. The victims had been Sarah Smith and James Thomas, and the story began on 21 March, when Mr Smith, Sarah Smith's husband, told Harley off for failing to prepare dinner for James Thomas and William Cox, two other men in his employment. He said to Harley that if she could not do her job reliably and punctually, she would be replaced. This infuriated Harley, who told James Thomas the next morning that she could not stand the sight of her master

and that, given the opportunity, she would gladly poison him. Later that same day, Harley was sent by her mistress to Bishops Castle to buy a few items. When she returned, she accounted for all the money her mistress had given her, claiming she had kept a penny for herself in payment. Then came the fateful day of 23 March, when Harley woke early to make some coffee. After drinking it, James Thomas and Sarah Smith became extremely ill. They died shortly afterwards. Later, a chemist by the name of Blunt would analyse the coffee and discover in it a penny's worth of arsenic, enough of it to kill two people. Despite all the evidence against Harley, the jury returned a verdict of not guilty. In summing up, the judge expressed his hope that she was in fact innocent – and added that if she was not, she should thank the Almighty that she had been blessed with such luck.

Death by arsenic is a gruesome fate. As soon as someone consumes the poison, they begin to suffer headaches, drowsiness and diarrhoea. After the poison has been in your body for longer, convulsions are common, as is blood in your urine, vomiting, muscle cramps, extreme stomach pain and hair loss. Internally, your kidneys, lungs and liver are all being destroyed due to cell death and haemorrhages. Arsenic interrupts the cellular process which produces ATP, a molecule that transports energy through the body's cells. Without ATP, your cells can't perform the tasks they need and begin to starve. This all leads to either a coma or death.

12 AUGUST 1829 Charles Rose was indicted in Shrewsbury on this day for stealing a black mare from George Rutter on 17 March. At the time this offence was usually punishable by death. The perpetrators of such a crime were often adult males, either in their late twenties or thirties. They were also usually men with agricultural jobs, as opposed to hardened criminals. The lure of this crime might seem unclear in this day and age, especially considering the high price the criminal would have to pay if caught. However, such a crime could reap a significant monetary profit once the horses were sold. Luckily for Rose, the judge must have been feeling either very lenient or particularly cheerful on this day, as he spared Rose the capital punishment and instead transported him for life.

13 AUGUST 1836 Laurence Curtis and Patrick and Edward Donneley were executed on this day in front of Shrewsbury Gaol for the crime of robbing and violently beating Thomas Woodward, a malt mill maker, and Thomas Urwick, his nephew, on 23 March at Loppington. The sentence came after the trial on 1 August, which was held in front of Mr Justice Littledale. The men stole £25 in notes, £9 in coins and silver, a silk handkerchief and a watch from the two men. The 'penny dreadful', a small illustrated booklet which was sold at public executions and usually retained as a souvenir, also added that they took away 'four half crowns, a shilling, and a sixpence.' The penny dreadfuls on sale at these executions were usually printed by Waidson, and were highly dramatised. This particular one opened with the following: 'Death is the most awful event which the sons of men are called either to witness or experience, and when we behold an ignominious termination of life surrendered to the offended laws of our country, it is most affecting of all spectacles.'

14 AUGUST 1829 News broke that John Nodin was indicted and charged with feloniously assaulting Eliza Cuerton (21), resulting in a death sentence being imposed. Cuerton had been the object of Nodin's affections for several months when, on the 17 June, he paid her a late-night visit. Her parents had recently gone to bed and Cuerton was about the do the same when she heard a knock at the door. From the floor above, Cuerton opened a window to see who the visitor was, and recognised Nodin instantly. He asked her to come down and let him in. Cuerton refused at first, but Nodin was extremely persistent. Despite her instincts, Cuerton eventually came downstairs and opened the door. Nodin then suggested a walk. She replied that it was far too late at night to go out. In response, Nodin forced his way into the house and slammed the door behind him. He then pushed his lover into the parlour, and threw her to the floor. Cuerton screamed – with the hope of attracting her sleeping parents' attention – but her screams were soon quelled by Nodin. It took fifteen minutes for her mother to hear the clamour downstairs; when she rose to see what was happening, Nodin ran. For a number of days Cuerton was unable to leave her bed. He came to visit

once, to ask how she was and if she had told her father what had transpired. He then begged her not to go to the police, trying to convince her that his behaviour, though unfavourable, should not cost him his life. She ignored him, sending him to his death.

15 AUGUST 1795 John Urquhart (alias John Smith) was executed at the new drop in Shrewsbury. He was hanged for the crime of shoplifting, and seemed extremely penitent. The *Salopian Journal* said of Urquhart, 'he was a young man of strong natural parts improved by good education, but his bad company proved his ruin.'

16 AUGUST 1828 Ann Harris became the last woman to be publicly hanged in Shrewsbury on this date. The crime she was hanged for was that of being an accessory to the murder of James Harrison. James Harrison was a petty criminal in Market Drayton, and was strangled by John Cox and Joseph Pugh while Robert Cox, John's little brother, kept an eye out to ensure their privacy. After the deed was done, they buried the body. The reasoning for Harrison's demise is somewhat complex, and involved the fact that Harrison was a chief witness for the prosecution against a young thief by the name of Thomas Ellison – who was Ann Harris' son, and the Coxes' brother-in-law. The plan was to get Harrison out of the picture so Ellison would not be hanged for the crime of sheep stealing. Ann Harris bribed the Cox brothers to commit the murder, knowing that when the trial finally came around the chief witness wouldn't be present to testify (and therefore there would be insufficient grounds to carry on with the trial). The case would have to be dropped. All may well have gone according to plan for Ellison if not for the fact that his thieving ways soon saw him facing brand new charges, this time of stealing fowls. In an attempt to spare himself the gallows, Ellison spilled the beans on his own mother and his brothers-in-law. Ann Harris was the first woman to be hanged in a quarter of a century, and it is estimated that 5,000 people attended the execution. Her body was spared dissection and she was allowed a burial.

17 AUGUST 1816 It was reported on this day that an ancient tomb in St Mary's Church, Shrewsbury, was removed into the chancel. The tomb was decorated with a figure of a cross-legged knight, with a lion at his feet. When the tomb was opened and explored, some leg and thigh bones, along with a skull, were discovered. They were believed to have come from two adults and a child. The men kept digging and when they reached the bottom they found a coffin, containing an extremely well-preserved skeleton, measuring 5ft 3in. The body was wrapped in leather and was missing a head. The workers looked around for this missing body part but could not find it. Identities for the skeleton included names such as Roger Leybourne, who fought for King Henry III against the Earl of Leicester in 1263, and Henry 'Hotspur' Percy (who had died in the Battle of Shrewsbury after lifting up his visor to get some air).

18 AUGUST 1930 Alice Gatensbury of Peplow Farm, Market Drayton, died in Whitchurch Cottage Hospital after being knocked down by a van the previous day. On the day in question, she had received a lift from her son. She was run over by the van as she got out of his car to visit a friend's home and attempted to cross the street.

19 AUGUST 1841 An attempted murder took place at the Angel Inn, Ludlow, on this day. The criminal was Joseph Misters (25) from Birmingham, who intended to cut the throat of a John Ludlow, a cattle salesman who often carried large amounts of money with him for business purposes. Misters seemingly put a lot of thought and effort into his plan. After following Ludlow and getting to know his routine, he determined that Ludlow was a man of habit, and always stayed in the same rooms when he visited the Angel Inn. He hid in Ludlow's favoured room, where he resolved to wait until Ludlow fell asleep, when he would put his murderous plan into action. He got out a razor and tried to slit the throat of the man sleeping, completely helpless, in the bed. Unfortunately for Misters, Ludlow had deviated from tradition and was staying in an altogether different room.

The inhabitant was instead William Mackreth, another travelling businessman. When Mackreth felt the razor touch his face he jumped instantly out of bed, despite having already been cut quite badly with the razor. Mackreth ran from his room and was soon admitted to the Royal Salop Infirmary, where his injury left him unable to talk. The medical staff assumed that Mackreth had tried to commit suicide, but he was eventually able to get his hands on some paper and let them know what happened. Joseph Misters of Birmingham was found guilty of attempted murder and sentenced to be hanged. Following his execution, *The Times* reported that 'the roads in the neighbourhood were crowded with persons carousing and enjoying themselves, as if returning from the sports of a racecourse, the awful scene they had so lately witnessed being rather a subject of merry observation than solemn reflection and awful warning.'

20 AUGUST 1349 John Le Strange of Whitchurch, who had already lost his son Humphry to the same fate, died on this day of the Black Death. Before the inquest into his death began on 30 August, John's eldest son also succumbed to the disease.

21 AUGUST 1861 A driver by the name of John James Bailey (9) suffered a horrible accident on this day. He worked for the Old Park Colliery in Wellington and was crushed between the sides of two skips.

22 AUGUST 1887 A roadman by the name of Smith (60) was working with the Lilleshall Co. in a small village named St George's (originally 'Pains Lane'). While on duty, two bars that were helping hold up the roof where Smith was working somehow became dislodged, causing the entire roof to fall on top of him, crushing him to death.

23 AUGUST 1901 On this day, at 2 a.m., a terrible train crash occurred at Market Drayton station. A train, after letting passengers off at Audlem, was returning to Wolverhampton when it crashed heavily into a goods train. Nearby witnesses immediately rushed to the scene to assist those on-board.

Thankfully, no one lost their lives – the driver and the stoker were extremely fortuitous in this. The driver was found relatively unharmed under a mountain of debris, and the stoker suffered only a small concussion.

24 AUGUST 1935 The body of Caroline Carver was found in the Shropshire Union Canal, a site that has seen its share of crime and death over the years. A local farmer attested that he had seen Caroline with her husband, Charles, earlier that night, and that they had been arguing heatedly. The usual signs and symptoms that are associated with drowning were present, but there was no other evidence to suggest that she had been held under water or thrown into the canal. As the only evidence linking Charles to the death came from the aforementioned farmer, and as the locals defended his character he was found not guilty. Caroline Carver's death still remains a mystery.

25 AUGUST 1791 William Gough was executed for the murder of Ann Brown of Lyndam, five days after he was sentenced. His execution took place at the Old Heath, and his body was then given to the surgeons to be anatomised. The bodies of murderers were, more often than not, promptly given to surgeons to be dissected following their executions. Dissection was in fact mentioned in the Murder Act of 1751, which read:

> Whereas the horrid crime of murder has of late been more frequently perpetrated than formerly ... it is thereby became necessary, that some further terror and peculiar mark of infamy be added to the punishment of death ... shall be immediately conveyed by the sheriff ... to the hall of the Surgeon's Company ... and the body delivered ... shall be dissected and anatomised by the said surgeons ... in no case whatsoever the body of any murderer shall be suffered to be buried, unless after such body shall have been dissected and anatomised as aforesaid.

The hope was that if criminals were denied a respectable burial and their corpses were publically dissected, it would prove to be a persuasive deterrent to crime. As there was no real way to preserve the dead bodies, anatomisation had to be performed quickly and was sometimes conducted immediately, in view of the public. This act, which seems barbaric in the eyes of modern society, was finally brought to an end with the Anatomy Act (1832), which only allowed unclaimed bodies from prisons and workhouses to be anatomised.

26 AUGUST 1870 The death of a young workman by the name of John Cotton was reported by the media on this day. The incident occurred near Shrewsbury railway station, on a bridge where two train lines coincided. Cotton was crossing this bridge when he saw a train approaching. He was quick-witted enough to step aside, but he unfortunately stepped into further danger as an express train from London was at that very second speeding into Shrewsbury station on the other line. He was knocked down and nearly cut in two after the carriages passed over him. Amazingly, he held out for long enough to be escorted to the Royal Salop Infirmary, but he died soon after his admittance.

27 AUGUST 1832 While attempting to break up a fight in Mardol, a few watchmen were forced to restrain a number of men. One man suddenly wrenched himself away, ran towards the Severn and jumped in to swim away. Although at first the man appeared to be a skilled swimmer, his attempts at escape were foiled by his braces, which had burst open during the brawl: his trousers fell around his feet under the water and dragged him down until he drowned.

28 AUGUST 1887 Catherine Scragg of the Shrewsbury Board of Schools was returning to Shrewsbury on the train when she became a victim of a vicious assault between Wellington and Shrewsbury. Shortly after leaving Wellington, a man, who had been the only other passenger in her compartment, approached her and began an assault that was only interrupted thanks to a gentleman who witnessed the act from an adjoining compartment and intervened.

29 AUGUST 1940 Early in the morning on this day, Ken Ritchie (7) of Bridgnorth was awakened by a loud noise, which he soon recognised as a high-pitched whistle. He was thrown from his bed seconds later by what turned out to be a German bomb. The bomb destroyed his home, but he managed to avoid being a victim of the Blitz on Bridgnorth. His sister Lorna was fortunately away on holiday, as the ceiling of her bedroom completely collapsed onto her bed, meaning that she almost certainly would have been killed. Years later, the bomb site became a memorial garden dedicated to the victims in the area that died on this day.

30 AUGUST 1811 On this day *The Times* reported on the execution of John Taylor, James Baker, William Turner, Isaac Hickman and Abraham Whitehouse, who were hanged on 24 August in front of the gaol for the burglary of Mr Norcop's house at Betton. Before the hanging, the five were engaged in prayer by the chaplain. Having received the sacrament, Hickman and Baker fell to their knees in prayer while on the scaffold. Taylor and Turner spoke softly but regretfully about how they had behaved. Whitehouse was the only one who remained completely silent throughout the proceeding.

31 AUGUST 1920 At a perilous corner of the Holyhead road, between Shrewsbury and Bicton, two cars crashed into each other. Commander Cecil of Bangor had been driving one car, with his wife in the passenger seat. They were badly injured and taken to the Royal Salop Infirmary. Reverend Lamb of Rugby had also been in the car, but was unharmed. The occupants of the opposing car were Major and Mrs King of Ford and their daughter Violet, who suffered no serious injury.

SEPTEMBER

Human skulls. (Wikimedia Commons)

1   SEPTEMBER 1939 In this month, rural Shropshire saw an influx of people fleeing from cities that had a high risk of bombing. Many of the evacuees came from Birmingham, Liverpool, the Wirral, and Manchester. Although it was certainly in their best interests, this move was often traumatic for a lot of the children, as many of them had been sent independently of their families and knew there was a chance they would never see them again.

2   SEPTEMBER 1889 Henry Slack was mowing grass in Whixall Moss on this day when he made an unexpected discovery: a collection of human bones. Intrigued, Slack started digging and found that there were many more than he originally thought. Slack contacted Superintendent Edwards and Sergeant Griffiths of Whitchurch and the following day they attended the scene and found the almost perfect remains of a male skeleton. There still remained flesh on the breast bone, abdomen and thighs. The flesh and bones were both oddly blackened, and it was estimated that the body had been buried at this spot for a considerable amount of time.

3   SEPTEMBER 1935 A miner by the name of Frederick Herbert from Gledrid Chirk Bank, Oswestry, was working at Ifton Colliery when he was killed suddenly by the fall of a rock that landed on his head. Ifton, originally known as the Gertrude Mine, was once the largest coal mine in the county and employed in excess of 1,300 men. The pit finally closed in 1968 as a result of several fires.

4   SEPTEMBER 1928 A possible case of anthrax presented itself in a cow on Thomas Union's farm. The farm was located in Hordley Grange, Ellesmere, and the case was confirmed by an official of the Ministry of Agriculture. The cow's body was promptly destroyed. Anthrax often affects cattle and sheep, and people who interact with the infected animals can often contract the disease. Infection, caused by bacteria, commonly involves respiratory collapse, black boils and gastro-intestinal difficulties. Untreated, the mortality rate after contracting anthrax is approximately 92 per cent.

5 **SEPTEMBER** 1789 This day saw the double execution of Thomas Phipps Senior (48) and Thomas Phipps Junior (20). The duo had been found guilty of printing and issuing a counterfeit £20 note. The crime may seem to be far from exciting, but their hangings turned into a very dramatic affair. After the guilty verdict was passed, and it was too late for reprieve, Phipps Junior confessed that his father had taken no part in the crime, and was not even aware that the crime was being committed. When they were taken to the gallows, Phipps Senior was reported to have said to his child, 'Tommy, thou hast brought me to this shameful end, but I forgive thee,' to which Thomas Junior made no answer. He then said, 'Thou hast brought me hither; dost thou lead the way?' Thomas Junior ascended the gallows first, but his father soon walked up to meet him. They were hanged simultaneously and in the final few moments before the bolt was drawn the father and son embraced each other. The newspapers at the time claimed that they dropped to their deaths still locked in an embrace, provoking a huge wave of sympathy from the onlookers.

6 **SEPTEMBER** 1651 The Battle of Worcester, on 3 September, proved to be a disaster for the Royalist army. Subsequently, Charles II and his remaining forces fled the scene and Cromwell placed a £1,000 bounty

on his head. If Charles II had been found, he would probably have met his death in much the same manner as Charles I, but one of Charles' attendants discovered a place where the future king could hide in safety for some time: Boscobel House, situated near Telford. When Charles arrived, his hair was cut in an effort to disguise him, and his skin was rubbed with dirt in an attempt to make him look like a commoner. On this day William Carlis (his name is given as Careless by some sources) suggested that the king should hide in an oak tree in the woods near Boscobel house. There, he argued, the king would be less likely to be found than anywhere else in the house. This is where the king took refuge, with some beer, bread and cheese. At one point during his hideout a Roundhead passed right beneath the tree but fortunately he failed to notice the king, who was hovering just above his head. Sadly this tree has been destroyed over time, due, in part, to the fact that many of its visitors have taken a piece as a memento. However, another tree has been grown from one of its acorns in the same location.

Charles II was offered a hiding spot in the form of the Boscobel Oak, where he avoided the fate of Charles I. (Sjwells53, Wikimedia Commons)

7 SEPTEMBER 1896

A labourer for the Hollinswood Ballast Hill Colliery by the name of William Underwood (49) became yet another man to lose his life in the dangerous mining trade. This particular fatal and gruesome incident occurred when Underwood became stuck between a cage and a slag crusher. The combined force and weight of the two objects eventually crushed him to death.

8 **SEPTEMBER** 1953 The body of Edward Barclay (13), a resident of Duddleston Heath near Ellesmere, was recovered after a fire broke out in a Dutch farm at Dussleston. Apparently the Shropshire native had been helping the owners with the harvesting. In the confusion and chaos caused by the outbreak of the fire, no one noticed that the boy was missing until it was far too late.

9 **SEPTEMBER** 1861 Five young men died on this day. They were all miners for the Donnington Colliery and were working in Wellington when the flat chain in the machinery broke, killing all of them. The deceased were brothers Thomas (23) and Henry Swift (19) and William Worral (36). Thomas Foulke and Thomas Davies, who were both just 14 at the time of the accident, also sadly passed away.

10 **SEPTEMBER** 1834 The year 1968 saw the birth of a new town in the county of Shropshire. It was named in honour of Thomas Telford, the noted civil engineer and architect, who died after growing severely ill with a bilious derangement. His death was prolonged and finally occurred on 2 September. The funeral took place on this day, where testimony described Telford as having 'the most genial disposition'. He was 'a delightful companion, his laugh was the heartiest I ever heard; it was a pleasure to be in his society.'

11 **SEPTEMBER** 1856 The town of Shrewsbury was inundated with crowds, and decorated with banners, flags and evergreens during a display to honour Colonel Percy Egerton Herbert, quartermaster general of the Crimean Army, as well as the other Shropshire officers who served or lost their lives in the war. The Crimean War began in October 1853 and lasted for nearly three years. During this time, the United Kingdom lost a great number of soldiers. In total, approximately 21,000 people died. Nearly 3,000 were killed in action and 2,000 died of wounds. A staggering 16,000 died of disease. During this time, Herbert was invaluable and, due to his efforts and his services during the war, he received knighthoods from

various governments including the French, Turkish and Sardinian. He was also made an aide-de-camp to Queen Victoria. Herbert settled in Styche, Market Drayton, after marrying Lady Mary Petty Fitzmaurice on 4 October 1960. He remained in Market Drayton until he died, at 54 years of age, on 7 October 1876. He was buried at Moreton Say and his widow, Lady Herbert, lived for a further fifty years.

12 SEPTEMBER 1857 Ann 'Nanny' Morgan (who was sometimes known by her alias, Evans) was murdered on this date by William Davies, a labourer who lived with her in her cottage at Westwood. There was a significant age difference between the two, with Morgan being 65 and Davies around 30. Due to this, rumours were ripe in Much Wenlock that Morgan had concocted some sort of spell or potion and that Davies was under her thrall. Others said that Davies stayed with her with the hope that he might inherit all her money when she finally passed on. There was a decent amount to inherit. Morgan did well financially, and earned money by making potions. As such, she had earned a reputation as a witch, prompting a degree of fear in those who knew her. People claimed the woman had the 'evil-eye' and was able to tell fortunes, a trade she learned from gypsies. Respectable ladies and servants alike would visit Morgan from miles around to listen to their futures. Contrary to the general dislike for Morgan amongst the locals, people generally liked Davies and were aware of the fact they argued regularly. On the day of her death Morgan sent Davies to Much Wenlock with some money, which she told him to use to buy some meat. On his way he stopped first at the Bulls Head pub and then the Horse and Jockey for a few drinks. When Davies returned, and Morgan found out how he had actually spent her money, it prompted a massive fight which led to him packing his things, including a watch Morgan had given him. This in turn prompted yet another argument over who deserved to keep the watch – an argument that quickly spiralled into murder. When her mutilated body was found, the woman was still clutching the watch in her hand. Morgan had been impaled with an eel spear, and her carotid artery had been severed. When the fugitive lover was eventually arrested, he looked extremely confused and tired, and is known to have said, 'I did love that old woman'. During Davies' trial, no word was said in Morgan's favour, with all the sympathy going to Davies. Davies was ultimately found guilty, but the traditional death penalty was withheld due to the extenuating circumstances discussed in court. Instead, he was transported for life but, after an accident (attributed to Morgan's evil-eye), his ship sank on the journey to Australia. Morgan's reputation as a witch has continued till this day, where the story has been elaborated and now includes new details, such as the claim that she owned two cats named 'Hell's Breath' and 'Hell's Fire'.

13 SEPTEMBER 1875 The media reported on an inquest into a colliery accident which had occurred on 11 September. On the day in question, eleven miners died at the Donnington Wood Colliery of the Lilleshall Coal, Iron and Engineering Co. The miners descended the pit as planned, and were followed by a horse that was lowered down to them. When the workers on the surface realised that no one below had received the horse, they began to shout down to their workmates. They received no reply. Not long after, many men descended the same pit, willing to risk their lives to find out what had happened. The inquest revealed that part of the pit had fired and filled with a toxic gas, which acted instantly. The inquest resulted in a verdict of 'accidental death'.

14 SEPTEMBER 1825 Enoch Long was run over by John Abbott's cart and killed on this date. Abbott was tried in March the following year, but as he was given 'a good character for humanity', he received only a year in prison (with hard labour) for causing the accident.

15 SEPTEMBER 1923 It was determined by the Ministry of Agriculture that a cow from George Lewis Hitchen's Stanwardine Park Farm in Baschurch was suffering from foot-and-mouth disease, following an outbreak amongst his sheep the preceding week. This occurrence took place twenty-six years after the first ever recorded case. On 18 September, inspectors decided that the best course of action was to cull the whole herd, including sixty-eight cattle, fifty-nine sheep and twenty-six pigs.

16 SEPTEMBER 1936 A well-known farmer by the name of Frederick James Dickens was killed in Wem. The accident occurred when Dickens was following a horse and cart that was being driven by his young son. At one point in the ride, his son picked up a gun and it discharged. The shot killed Dickens almost instantly.

17 SEPTEMBER 1921 Edwin William Peach, a boot manufacturer of Stafford, was involved in a road accident in Shrewsbury on this date that resulted in the deaths of Richard Watkins, John Lewis Bufton and William Alfred Williams. Peach was committed to the Shrewsbury Assizes on the charge of manslaughter. He protested his innocence, insisting that he was sober at the time, was not driving faster than 15mph, and had been driving for twenty years without incident. Peach claimed that the accident must have occurred after his foot slipped: instead of breaking, he hit the accelerator. The jury concluded that although they believed the driver to be negligent, there existed insufficient evidence to uphold a verdict of manslaughter, and Peach was acquitted.

18 SEPTEMBER 1591 This day saw the conclusion of a particularly busy assizes at Shrewsbury. On the 16th, 17th and 18th, sixty prisoners were tried. Twenty of these prisoners were condemned. Ten prisoners were reprieved and one woman was reprieved due to the efforts of other women in the town. Of these sixty prisoners, eight were ultimately hanged at Old Heath. One of them, Edward Nixon, was hanged in chains for the crime of murder.

In September 1591, Shrewsbury saw sixty prisoners tried, eight of which were hanged at the Old Heath. (Library of Congress, LG-DIG-ppmsc-08836)

19 SEPTEMBER 1929 A fire erupted at Soulton Hall, near Wem. The blaze destroyed more than 200 tons of corn and clover, but thankfully the farm buildings were able to be saved.

20 SEPTEMBER 1642 Charles I issued the Wellington Declaration on this day which promised to preserve the Protestant religion and liberties of his people. Charles then travelled from Wellington to Shrewsbury to meet his two sons, Charles and James, as well as Prince Rupert and other noblemen to establish a mint in the town. He remained in the town until 12 October, when he moved on to Bridgnorth and Edge Hill. Here, the first battle of the Civil War (the Battle of Edge Hill) was fought. During this pitched battle, the wounded on both sides amounted to approximately 1,500 men, and a further 500 died. The matter of who won is still debated, but both sides fought fiercely into the night. It is apparently thanks to the extremely low temperature of that particular night that so many of the

King Charles I travelled to Shrewsbury in 1642 to meet his sons. Soon after, the first battle of the Civil War began. (THP)

wounded survived: the freezing weather encouraged blood clotting and prevented infection, saving countless lives.

21 SEPTEMBER 1947 An inquest was held on the body of Henry Temple Robins, who had been the rector of Chetwynd. He died on 17 September in the Eye, Ear and Throat Hospital after drinking a bottle of what he believed to be sacramental wine, but which in fact contained sodium hydroxide. The inquest revealed that Robins' mouth and throat were badly burned. Sodium hydroxide, also known as caustic soda or lye, is a white solid alkali that comes in flakes or granules. It is widely used in cleaning products and is easily dissolved in water or alcohol. Although it is not usually extremely toxic, it is very corrosive. If consumed, a fatal amount could be as little as a few millilitres. Once you have been exposed to sodium hydroxide the natural reaction is to desperately try to wash it off due to the extreme pain it can cause. This pain is due mostly to tissue destruction. Robins likely experienced a fierce burning sensation in his mouth and stomach as his lips and tongue began to swell. It is common for victims to vomit as the body tries to rid itself of the alkali, with dead pieces of skin being found in the substance. Robins' heartbeat would probably have sped up to a dangerous pace, accompanied by clammy skin. The sodium hydroxide would ultimately have corroded his lungs, larynx and stomach too badly for him to recover.

22 **SEPTEMBER** **1913** A car accident occurred, with five people receiving serious injuries. The accident took place near Market Drayton at Ternhill, where the two main roads from London to Holyhead and Market Drayton to Shrewsbury intersect. One of the cars, driven by Clark Gaskell of Wolverhampton, was completely overturned. Fortunately for everyone involved, Dr Broughton of Langley Green was riding his motorcycle home from Llandudno at the time and was able to tend to the injured parties before further medical assistance could be procured. Injuries included severe wounds and a fractured clavicle (broken collarbone).

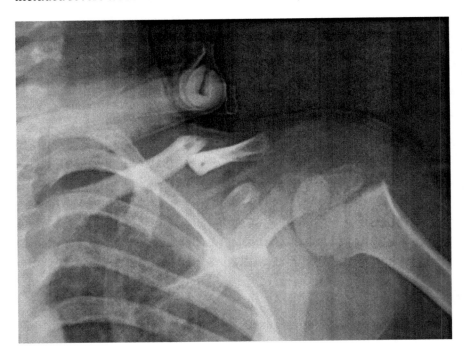

One of the injuries procured following a car accident in Market Drayton was a clavicle fracture in 1913. (Nevit Dilmen, Wikimedia Commons)

23 **SEPTEMBER** **1459** This rainy Sunday morning saw the Battle of Blore Heath, the first major battle of the Wars of the Roses. A 'parlay' was attempted before the fight began, in a traditional attempt to avoid unnecessary violence. Needless to say, the attempt was unsuccessful. The

battle was fought at Ludlow between the Houses of Lancaster and York and lasted the rest of the day and into the night. As was traditional in medieval battles, the fight began with an archery duel. It is believed that the Lancastarians lost approximately 2,000 men. Estimations regarding Yorkist deaths vary, with some believing that as few as 100 men were killed, although others believe that a figure of 1,000 is more probable. Even now, a stone cross stands on this site in Blore Heath as a tribute to Audley, the Lancastrian leader, who lost his life during the fight. According to local legend, Hempmill Brook apparently ran red with blood for three whole days after the battle came to an end.

Legend also suggests that Queen Margaret of Anjou was in the spire of the nearby Mucklestone church tower and witnessed the whole battle. She then made her escape when it became clear that the House of Lancaster had lost, and that Lord Audley had been defeated. She found a blacksmith by the name of William Skelhorn and paid him to reverse the shoes on her horse so that she could cover her escape. The battle is re-enacted each year at the same location.

24 SEPTEMBER 1894 On 20 July of this year, Daniel Walters (64) suffered a terrible accident while working in the town of Donnington. Walters was a repairer, and on the day in question was working for the Barn Colliery of the Lilleshall Co. Due to a certain amount of negligence, the roof that he was working on had not been timbered properly. He fell off and suffered a back injury and a broken thigh. Injuries such as these were far more serious back in the nineteenth century, as the doctors were not as able to treat the ailments as we are today. Broken thigh bones, in particular, would have been very difficult to remedy because of the muscles around this particular area: they are generally very strong, so quite a lot of manipulation is required in order to stretch them into the right place; this is needed so the bone can be set in its natural position. Of course, this was all done in a time before antiseptic, when amputation was a common solution to a compound fracture. His injuries grew progressively worse, and Daniel died on this day.

25 SEPTEMBER 1917 A fire broke out at Church Farm, Welsh Hampton, which caused damage to the tune of several thousands of pounds. Even though the Ellesmere and Oteley Fire Brigades were only 3 miles away, the horse-drawn fire service was not able to reach the scene until almost three hours had elapsed.

26 SEPTEMBER 1849 On the week commencing 26 September, two deaths caused by cholera and one death caused by diarrhoea in the town of Market Drayton were reported to the General Board of Health. Cholera, caused by the bacteria *Vibrio colerae*, is an infection of the small intestine. Intense diarrhoea and vomiting are common symptoms. The infection is transmitted mainly by drinking or eating from a source that contained the faeces of another infected person. The extent of the diarrhoea and vomiting, more often than not, leads to dehydration and an electrolyte imbalance; sometimes in excess of 50 litres can be lost. This dehydration can cause death if not immediately treated, and this normally happens when 10 to 15 per cent of the person's original body weight is lost. Depending on the severity of the condition, the whole process might take less than a few hours.

27 SEPTEMBER 1864 A tragedy occurred today when nine miners lost their lives at the Brick Kiln Leasow pit in Madeley. The incident occurred when a skip became detached while coming back up the shaft. To make the incident even more heart-breaking, four of the miners were younger than 16, and two others were only 18 years old. The miners were later buried in one grave at Madeley church. 2,500 people attended the funeral, the majority of whom were fellow miners and their families. The names of these miners were: Edward Wallett (52), who left behind four children; John Tranter (37), who left behind five children; Benjamin Davies (35); Joseph Maiden (18); William Jarrett (18); John Jones (14); John Farr (14); Francis Cookson (13); and William Onions (12).

28 SEPTEMBER 1803 Ralph Griffiths, who was born in Shropshire, founded and became the editor of London's first successful literary magazine,

The Monthly Review. This publication persevered until 1845. He eventually became blind, but carried on his role as editor of his beloved magazine until he died on this day.

29 SEPTEMBER 1865 On this day *The Times* reported on the case against William George, alias Morgan, who had been charged with persuading Thomas Farnell, alias 'the Bear', to violently beat Police Constable Davies. Davies had arrested him and at the time was escorting him to prison. George received one month in prison with hard labour, and Davies remained in hospital, extremely ill and with little hope of recovery.

30 SEPTEMBER 1645 Parliamentarian Sir Thomas Mytton became the High Sherriff of Shropshire on this date, and was often known afterwards as Major-General Mytton. Along with Colonel Michael Jones, Mytton went on to defeat Sir William Vaughan, the famous Royalist, just outside Denbigh. This act ultimately dashed Royalist hopes to relieve Chester. Mytton died in London eleven years later and was subsequently returned to Shrewsbury, to be interred in St Chad's Church.

Following his death, Sir Thomas Mytton was interred in St Chad's Church, Shrewsbury. (Photo by Samantha Lyon)

OCTOBER

Ludlow Castle. (Library of Congress, LC-DIG-ppmsc-08629)

1   OCTOBER **1908** On this day the mayor was presented a scarlet cloak by the Walcott family of Bitterley Court. The cloak was the one that Charles I wore at his execution on 30 January 1649. It was promptly put on display at the Shrewsbury Museum. The historic cloak, which remains in good condition, had been retrieved by William Walcott, who was a page to the king and was with him at the scaffold.

2   OCTOBER **1911** After suffering a seizure, Revd T.J. Rider, the vicar of Baschurch, fell from his horse near Wem and broke his neck. Seizures are generally caused by a disturbance in the electrical activity of the brain. The vicar was well loved and held in high esteem throughout the county.

3   OCTOBER **1283** Dafydd ap Gruffydd (45) had been the Prince of Wales for less than a year when he was executed. Dafydd was tried on 30 September and saw out his punishment on this day for high treason against King Edward I of England. The king stipulated that Dafydd's death was to be long and excruciating, so the ultimate sentence of being 'hanged, drawn and quartered' was passed. He was dragged on the ground through Shrewsbury while attached to a horse. He was then hanged, revived, and disembowelled whilst still conscious, before having his entrails burned before his eyes. This barbaric form of torture was not rendered completely obsolete in England until 1870. A man by the name of Geoffrey was reportedly paid 20*s* for carrying out much of the execution. Dafydd was the last independent ruler of Wales.

4   OCTOBER **1594** Election night disorders were described by many as 'a customary annual event'. However, in this year the disorder was so great that it resulted in the murder of Thomas Lacon, servant to Richard Cherwell, who perished on this night.

5   OCTOBER **1923** Following the death of Clement John Coffin, an ironmonger of Ellesmere, an inventory of his possessions was made. Amongst his effects was more than £1,000 in gold pieces, which were

secreted around his shop, as well as £3,000 in bank notes (found hidden in various containers). His lucky shop companion, Ernest Griffiths, was left every item in his will.

6 OCTOBER 1902 Having been discharged from the workhouse, John Davies saw his estranged wife in public and became increasingly riled by the 'silent treatment' she seemed to be giving him. When Mrs Davies saw him on Llys Lane, she ignored him and kept walking. Davies said to his friend, Mr Hughes, 'I don't know what's the matter with that bloody woman! She won't talk to me, but I will make her talk just now.' He then ran to catch up with her, and put an arm around her in an ostensibly friendly way. However, seconds later, passers-by witnessed an awful scene: as they watched, he stabbed his wife in the chest with a knife he had hidden inside his clothes. He then attacked her face so badly that the flesh was cut away from the skull. As soon as he realised what he had done, the husband looked horrified. He tried to commit suicide, but this desperate act was prevented by a local by the name of Thomas Owen. Afterwards, a distraught Davies kept muttering that he wanted 'to be left alone', and that he wanted to die. He quietly pled guilty at his trial at the Shropshire Assizes, where he was found guilty but insane.

7 OCTOBER 1961 Mr Justice Hinchliffe today ordered that medical writer Robert Boynton (48) be detained at Broadmoor. The sentence of thirty years, was handed down after Boynton was found guilty of three counts of attempted murder. He eventually died in the same hospital in 1994. The crimes were committed on the 2 and 7 August, and the victims were Arthur Rowlands, Robert Carswell and Robert William Roberts of the Shropshire Constabulary. Arthur Rowlands (39) was shot in the face at close range by Boynton. When Boynton saw Rowlands, he is reported to have remained frighteningly calm as he said, 'You should not have come. I am going to shoot you.' Although Rowlands miraculously survived, despite receiving seventy shotgun pellets, a cardboard wad and an air-cushion compressed wad to his face, he was permanently blinded.

8 OCTOBER **1927** Mary Webb (46), the Salopian romantic novelist and poet, passed away on this day. Webb had developed Graves' Disease at the age of 20, which caused her ill health and pain throughout her life. Morbidly enough, the aches and pains she suffered might well have enriched her writing and allowed her to artfully depict torment, both physical and emotional, in her writing. Her fiction continues to be well-loved and well-read in Shropshire today. Graves' Disease is an auto-immune disease which causes the thyroid to be overactive and produce a surplus of thyroid hormones. Goitre is a common symptom, as is vocal-cord paralysis, muscle degeneration, insomnia and an irregular heartbeat. It is also not uncommon for one or both of the eyes to protrude, and for the victim to get lumpy red skin on their lower legs.

9 OCTOBER **1885** An inquest was held on the body of William Last, gamekeeper to Colonel Lloyd of Aston Hall. He was shot on 8 October by Colonel Lloyd's son, Fitzwarren Lloyd. On the day in question Lloyd and a number of other gentlemen were shooting on the Middleton estate. Last had climbed a fence and was being followed by Lloyd, who tragically slipped on the fence, making his gun go off. The charge entered the victim's head, shattering it completely and causing instant death.

10 OCTOBER **1917** Farmers in Ellesmere were growing increasingly concerned after yet another outbreak of fire in the area. On this day the fire was at Bettisfield Hall Farm, and caused damage to the amount of £1,500. There had been five outbreaks of fire in the past two weeks, which made the farmers suspect that they were due to intentional malice. The Ellesmere Farmer's Association were this day offering £100 for the capture of the incendiaries, which is the equivalent of roughly £6,000 today.

11 OCTOBER **1942** John Henry Wainwright of Pipe Gate was driving his car in a blackout on this day when he accidentally crashed into an approaching cyclist. The cyclist was dead by the time Wainwright left his

vehicle, an experience made much worse when he discovered the cyclist was in fact his own father.

12 **OCTOBER 1867** Transportation was a once popular alternative to the death penalty. Using it meant that the criminal could be removed from 'respectable' society and had the added benefit of being relatively cheap. Prior to the American War of Independence of 1775, many criminals were sent to America and, from 1787, offenders were also sent to a penal colony at Botany Bay, Australia. Over the years, approximately 160,000 people were transported. Once they arrived at their locations, criminals were often required to work on projects such as road construction or mining. Transportation from Britain officially ended in 1868. The last ship to make the journey was the *Hougowmont*, which left on this day in 1867, arriving in Western Australia on 10 January 1868. John Jones of Shrewsbury was on this ship as punishment for the crime of burglary, serving a sentence of ten years.

13 **OCTOBER 1843** An accident occurred at Bletchley to one Mr H. Clive of Stych Hall as he was returning from a day of hunting. Clive was on his horse and approaching a low gate. When Clive stooped to open it, the horse decided to jump it: the action caused Clive to be thrown off, and the horse then landed on top of him. He was knocked unconscious, and remained so for about thirty minutes until he was discovered. Thankfully, medical help arrived quickly and he recovered well.

14 **OCTOBER 1822** *The Times* reported that Henry Andrews of Shrewsbury, who had served in a great number of battles during the Peninsular War, was on a 'sporting excursion' on the 12th, in a park near Oswestry, when he suffered a deadly accident. While reloading his double-barrel gun, Andrews nudged the trigger with his knee, causing it to discharge. The shot went straight into his head and killed him instantly.

15 **OCTOBER 1907** This day saw the occurrence of a horrible accident on the Shrewsbury rail, which was caused when the train operator

Following a tragic accident on the Shrewsbury railway, eighteen people were killed and a further sixty-one injured. (Photo by Samantha Lyon)

accidently sped up whilst approaching a dangerous curve on the rail. The train derailed, killing eighteen and injuring a further sixty-one.

16 OCTOBER 1877 A platelayer by the name of William Miles was killed on the Shrewsbury and Hereford railway on this day. The accident took place near Marshbrook station, when Miles moved from one line to another to allow a train to pass, and got run over by a goods train approaching on the other line. Miles left behind a wife and six children in Little Stretton.

17 OCTOBER 1877 An accident occurred on this day involving a young, 13-year-old 'hooker-on', whose name is recorded as 'Hayward'. Hayward was working in the Coalbrook Dale Colliery in Wellington when the fatal accident took place. While he was at the bottom of the pit, a basket of equipment was being lowered down for him to receive. Unfortunately, due to a fault in the chain, the basket fell and landed on him. The weight of

the equipment and the speed with which it fell meant that the poor worker was killed before any help could be procured.

18   OCTOBER 1826 On this day, local media reported on a serious accident involving Sir Tyrwhitt Jones. The accident occurred on 12 October: Jones was shooting in one of his manors near Shrewsbury when a bullet fired by another hunter entered his right eye. Incredibly, Jones survived, though he lost the use of the eye.

19   OCTOBER 1529 Richard Baker (sometimes also known as Richard Marciale, Richard Marshall and, mistakenly, as Richard Manners) was the penultimate abbot of Shrewsbury. He resigned as abbot in 1528 after sixteen years and became the prior of Morville on this date. During his time as prior, Baker began a scam that involved collecting funds without forwarding them on to the relevant authorities. This misdemeanour was eventually discovered, and Baker became involved in a Chancery court case that was brought forward by Thomas Butler, the new and final abbot. After the drama was lived out he settled down in Acton Arms, where he eventually died. Many believe he still haunts it as 'the White Man', and the pub is known as one of the most haunted in the county.

20   OCTOBER 1926 It was announced in the local media that the Lyon Memorial Hotel in Hodnet was being turned into an isolation hospital in order to deal with the growing number of diphtheria cases among the youth of the area. Up until this date those with the disease were sent to the Market Drayton Isolation Hospital, but it had reached full capacity and was unable to help any further patients. This was bad news for those who were infected, as the disease is a grim one. Symptoms usually begin anywhere from two to seven days after the patient initially becomes infected. Once this happens the patient will experience extreme fever, chills, fatigue and – on occasion – a 'bluing' of the skin. A sore throat is also a sign of the disease, causing incredible difficulty swallowing and sometimes even breathing. When the toxin that causes diphtheria spreads

to the blood, it becomes life threatening, affecting important organs such as the kidneys and the heart. Once this happens, around 50 per cent of patients will die.

21 OCTOBER 1898 Mr Gowan and his wife were indicted on this day at the Shropshire Quarter Sessions for the neglect and ill-treatment of their two orphan nieces, aged 9 and 12. The late parents had left Gowan £650 to ensure that their children would be well educated and looked after. To begin with, it appeared as if the girls were being treated fairly, like members of the family. Over time, however, the situation worsened and abuse became a regular occurrence. The National Society for the Prevention of Cruelty to Children became aware of the case and the court ordered for custody to be transferred to Revd Benjamin Waugh, the secretary to the society at the time. Gowan and his wife were both found guilty and sentenced to four months in prison with hard labour in the Shrewsbury Gaol, a sentence that most locals believed to be far too lenient.

22 OCTOBER 1941 After running out of fuel, two Czech pilots died after crashing into a field in Poynton Green. Although a local farmer had hurried to the scene in the hope of saving them, the fire was burning viciously by the time he reached the aircraft and he was unable to approach. It is often reported that this farmer saw a black cat saunter safely out of the aircraft and away from the flames. The cat was reportedly housed with an elderly local lady. After the lady died, the cat disappeared – but is said to reappear every decade on this day at the old crash site in Poynton Green.

23 OCTOBER 1799 The Tuckies Ferry accident at Jackfield occurred on this day. For reasons unknown, the ferry overturned with forty-one people onboard. Out of this number only thirteen survived the ordeal, the remaining twenty-eight having drowned. Some bodies were found the next morning, although they had drifted down the Severn quite a distance from the site. A number were not found for a whole month, and others were never found at all.

24 OCTOBER 1924 John Doughty (64), who was known by the locals as a solitary and quiet man, ran a grocer's shop on Sandford Avenue, Church Stretton. He lived in the rooms above with his wife Edith and daughter Kathleen (3). One day a few regulars noticed that the shop had not opened as usual and shortly after 9 a.m. a child heard groaning emanating from the back of the shop. When an errand boy arrived for work, he unlocked the shop and went round to the back – and found Doughty lying unconscious in the yard. The facts, as they later came out in court, showed that he had flung himself from the window above. Edith and Kathleen were discovered near a fireplace on an upper floor, alive but suffering from serious head injuries which eventually led to their deaths. A proceeding investigation showed no signs of forced entry as all the doors and windows had been locked from the inside. They did, however, discover a large, bloodied axe in the kitchen. Doughty was officially charged with their murders on this date, but was judged to be psychologically damaged and clinically insane. A search of the house revealed hundreds of unopened letters, the majority of which were unpaid bills, leaving him seriously in debt, the stress of which may have contributed to his mental instability. Throughout his trial his only contribution was to continually mutter, 'I don't remember doing it'. A verdict of guilty but insane was passed.

25 OCTOBER 1292 Robert Burnell, of Acton Burnell, who is known by some to have been the most important royal official of the thirteenth century, died on this day. During his time this bishop served as Lord Chancellor of England and even served as regent for a time after the death of King Henry III, when Edward was on crusade. He was also known for his scandalous personal life and he carried on an affair with a lady named Juliana, who reputedly gave birth to four of his sons. When he died he owned eighty-two manors, and an extremely important one to the Salopians is the Acton Burnell Castle, which he helped to build. Part of the castle is still intact in Acton Burnell, located extremely close to the local Concord College. The locals love the ghost stories that this ancient building has inspired, and on many occasions 'orbs' have reportedly been seen floating around the site.

26 OCTOBER 1956 On 22 October, Robert Crighton Wave (16), a pupil of Shrewsbury School, was found dead outside the main entrance of the main building. An estimated 34ft above the body was an open window, which prompted discussion over whether the death was a result of suicide. Major R.W.B. Crawford-Clarke, a coroner, said that although there were pointers to suicide, it may also have been an accident as the boy's teachers had said that the boy was in good spirits not long before his death. An inquest was held on this day, and an open verdict was returned.

A statue of Darwin, an ex-pupil of Shrewsbury School, is now situated outside Shrewsbury Library. (Photo by Samantha Lyon)

Robert Crighton Wave was found dead outside Shrewsbury School, now the site of the local library. (Photo by Samantha Lyon)

27 OCTOBER 1832 The *Salopian Journal* reported that their Royal Highnesses the Duchess of Kent and Princess Victoria, along with Sir John Conroy and Lady Catherine Jenkinson, were travelling from Whitchurch to Pitchford when a wheel fell off their coach, causing them to break down. The royal party was rescued by a local man who changed the wheel for them and helped them safely on their way.

28 OCTOBER 1959 A trench collapsed in Redhill, and Frank Jaundrell and Michael Callaghan were buried under the rubble. Their workmates acted quickly and tried their best to pull them to safety, but by the time they were reached, it was too late: the men had already passed on.

29 OCTOBER 1856 John Hollis, an unemployed waiter, lived with a young woman by the name of Anne Usher, sometimes better known as 'Annie Laurie'. The two had a sour history, and Hollis often mistreated Usher. He had been brought before the magistrates on more than one occasion and punished for his treatment of her. On this night, at approximately 10 p.m.,

Hollis was out in the Shrewsbury market square when he noticed Usher dancing with a man by the name of Clewett. Outraged, Hollis confronted her and asked what she thought she was doing. He was holding a knife at the time and might have stabbed her then and there had it not been for a man named Hopwood, who intervened at the right moment. Petrified, Usher struck out at Hollis a number of times before her lover was brought to the ground by a punch from a nearby man. Usher then ran away. When she reached the Plough Inn, she met a familiar face: a man she knew named Benjamin Bromley, who urged her to go home. She refused – she knew that when she got home she would have to deal with Hollis. Bromley stayed with her while she calmed down but, not long afterwards, Hollis found Bromley and Usher outside the pub – and he lost his temper once more. Once again he lifted his hand to her. This time she had a new defender: Bromley said they should, 'settle the matter like men'. This is where the story gets a bit surreal: both Bromley and Hollis had only one arm, and as such they decided that the fight would be fair. Hollis hit Bromley hard in the chest, and he immediately fell into the gutter. It was only as Hollis made his escape that the witnesses noticed that the lover had been holding a knife. Bromley was taken to the Royal Salop Infirmary, but eventually succumbed to the effects of a deep stab wound, measuring 0.75in, near the heart. Hollis, who had ditched the knife in the Severn in the interim, was captured near the Crow Inn in Frankwell.

30 OCTOBER 1823 An attempt was made on the once-beautiful Martha Mason's life on this day at Eyton, when a gun loaded with pieces of cut lead was fired at her. The shot entered the left side of her face, blinding her in the left eye. Although Mason (23) survived, she did not experience the same quality of life after the attack, finding it difficult even to open her mouth to eat.

31 OCTOBER Local legend says that if you are in Chirbury on Halloween at midnight, and walk around the church a dozen times, you will hear the names of all the villagers who are going to die in the subsequent year.

NOVEMBER

English Bridge, Shrewsbury. (Library of Congress, LC-DIG-ppmsc-08837)

1 NOVEMBER 1895 Alfred Lees (19), a driver for the Donnington Barracks, suffered an ultimately fatal accident on this day in Donnington. Lees was working at the time of the accident. Everything was running as usual until he dismounted the carriage to conduct certain checks, and the horse got spooked. In the chaos which ensued, as Lees desperately sought to calm the horse, it kicked him in the stomach. The kick ruptured an organ, causing peritonitis. Lees suffered for days before he died on 4 November. The peritoneum is a thin membrane which covers the inside of the abdomen, and also encloses most other abdominal organs. Peritonitis occurs when this becomes inflamed, usually when an organ suffers serious injury. This usually results in an infection. General symptoms include significant abdominal pain, which feels all the more intense when the sufferer moves, coughs, laughs or flexes the abdominal area. It is then not uncommon for the abdominal area to go extremely rigid, known as a 'washboard abdomen'. The sufferer will usually experience a fever, vomiting and nausea. Without the appropriate treatment, the average sufferer will survive for approximately twelve hours.

2 NOVEMBER 1873 On this day Edward Buckley and George Maddox, both severely wounded, were admitted to the Royal Salop Infirmary. The two had been at a house in Dorrington when one of them noticed a gun on top of a cupboard. After an amicable scuffle, not knowing that the gun was loaded, Buckley aimed the gun at Maddox and released the trigger. The charge entered directly into Maddox's face. A distraught Buckley immediately ran to fetch a local doctor before attempting to drown himself. Finding it impossible to do so, he instead slit his own throat with a pocket knife, partially severing the windpipe. Miraculously, due to prompt assistance and intervention, both men survived their injuries.

3 NOVEMBER 1902 On this day Richard Wigley (34), a butcher, walked 9 miles to Westbury to the Lion public house, stopping periodically for a drink or two. When he finally arrived at the pub, he found his girlfriend, Mary Ellen Bowen, grabbed her and dragged her into a darkened

passage. Bowen had been slowly but surely going off her boyfriend. Her letters to him were becoming fewer and farther between, and they seemed much less affectionate than they used to be. Wigley had become convinced that she was cheating on him. As Wigley dragged her along, Bowen managed to shout to a servant by the name of Ellen Richards; she begged her to contact the police. Sensing trouble, Wigley let her go. Bowen then returned to the pub, where she continued her waitressing, assuming the whole thing had blown over. Later in the night, however, her boss told her to go down to the basement to collect one or two things. There, in the dark, she was confronted once more by Wigley. He grabbed her by the arm and pushed her against the wall. He made such a commotion that the servant girl, Richards, overheard and was able to run for help. The last thing the servant saw as she ran was Wigley pulling a knife from his pocket and pressing it to Bowen's face. Bowen screamed for help – and then Wigley stabbed her in the throat. Afterwards, he reportedly said, 'I have done it, lads! I have done it for love. I had come on purpose to do it, and am ready to swing.' Wigley was sentenced to death on 18 March 1902, and his was the first execution in Shrewsbury for fourteen years. People say that Bowen's blood-stained handprint was impossible to remove, and remained on the cellar wall until the day the pub was demolished.

4 NOVEMBER 1918 Shropshire-born soldier Wilfred Owen is well known for his poetry, which described in great detail the terrible conditions of war, and how the battles of the First World War had affected the soldiers exposed to them. Far from glorifying war, Owen famously wrote about its unforgivable loss. He was killed in action on this day, during the crossing

of the Sambre-Oise Canal. One week later, almost to the hour, the church bells of Shrewsbury rang out to mark the final ceasefire just as the telegram containing the news reached his family. He was posthumously promoted to the rank of lieutenant the day after his death.

5   NOVEMBER 1821   Luke Oliver, William Griffiths, Daniel Williams and James Clarke were indicted on this day for breaking and entering Thomas Rodernhurst's home to commit burglary. From Rodernhurst's home in Cotton, the group stole a gun, money, snuff-boxes and other items. They were sentenced to death following a trial, and were told not to entertain any hopes of mercy.

6   NOVEMBER 1952   Britain experienced a vicious and extensive gale, the likes of which the country had not seen in years. At this time, the highest reported wind speed was 94mph at Shawbury.

7   NOVEMBER 1955   An announcement was made on this day regarding the progress of John Chetwynd-Talbott, 21st Earl of Shrewsbury (40), who was admitted into the Queen Elizabeth Hospital in Birmingham after his health began to deteriorate. He had extreme difficulty in breathing and, as such, had to be placed on an iron lung immediately. An iron lung is also known as a 'negative pressure ventilator' and helps patients who aren't able to exercise normal muscle control to breathe. Lord Shrewsbury was then given a diagnosis of acute poliomyelitis, most commonly known as polio. It is an infectious viral disease that is commonly spread from person to person via something known as the faecal-oral route. This is when pathogens in faecal particles are somehow ingested by another person. Symptoms of polio in the early stages of the disease include stiffness, especially in the neck or the back, muscle weakness, headache, fever, difficulty swallowing, irritability and a constant feeling of pins and needles. His wife, Nadine Muriel Crofton, remained by his bedside during his stay at the hospital.

8 NOVEMBER 1940 Lieutenant Eric Stanley Lock, who became known as 'Sawn-off Lock' due to his short height, was born in Bayston Hill on this day, and went on to become the RAF's most successful British pilot in the Battle of Britain. He was a skilled and brave fighter pilot, and first gained recognition for shooting down a twin-engine Messerschmitt Bf 110 that was leading a bomber formation at 20,000ft. On this day he further demonstrated his courage and resolution when his spitfire was damaged over Beachy Head, causing him to crash down into a ploughed field. Despite his extensive injuries, Lock managed to remove himself from the aircraft and walk away. He went missing in action the following year, on 3 August, when he flew to attack German soldiers near Calais. It is thought that Lock was shot down, but neither he nor his aircraft were ever found.

9 NOVEMBER 1844 An incident occurred this day on the Holyhead road, when a boat carrying Samuel Higginson, Edward Thomas, Thomas Birth and John Parry moored near the Montford Bridge. Police Constable Cumpstone saw the men cross the bridge shortly after 11 p.m., at which point they seemed friendly and sober. Not long afterwards, a man named George Whitehorn, who lived nearby, heard the sounds of fighting coming from the barge. He heard a combination of stamping feet and blows and the words, 'Fair rising, Ned,' but had no idea what the words meant. As it was late and extremely dark, he did not leave his house to investigate, but his conscience was eased when the noise died down soon afterwards. The following morning the crew announced that John Parry had gone missing without explanation – which was strange, as his hat, pipe and other items were still in the cabin of the boat. As the crew needed someone to navigate them back to Royal Hill, near Melverley, they hired a man named Richard Davies. During the journey back, Davies heard Edward Thomas express his doubt that Parry had just gone missing – he believed that he might have fallen overboard while in a drunken state. The men were questioned, but claimed that they'd spent the evening quietly smoking pipes. Following this, they said, they had gone to sleep and assumed Parry had done the same. Whether the men were ever really seriously suspected is unknown, but they

were never brought to court. The river was dragged, but Parry's body could not be found, and it is assumed that the body – if indeed the man had gone into the river – had been washed miles away. Parry left behind five children and a heavily pregnant wife.

10 NOVEMBER 1881 At Wellington, James Swinnerton was indicted for feloniously wounding his father with intent to murder. It is said that the father had been eating breakfast with his son when the latter, with no provocation whatsoever, picked up a razor and cut his father's throat. The father fought and managed to escape, despite being seriously wounded. During the trial, the father said that he believed Swinnerton was insane at the time and attested to the fact that in the past there had been talk of sending him to a mental asylum. Following a trial, James Swinnerton was found guilty and sentenced to twenty years' penal servitude.

11 NOVEMBER 1842 *The Times* reported two counts of wounding that occurred on the 9th in Ellesmere. On this day Edward Williams, Thomas Judson and Thomas Mason were in the town to watch a performer. At the time they appeared sociable and friendly. On the way home, however, a fight broke out between Mason and Williams. Williams' friend Judson noticed that he was getting quite angry and tried to convince him to go home and unwind. Unfortunately his attempts backfired horribly and Williams produced a knife and stabbed his friend in the abdomen. He then stabbed his chest, forehead and at the back of his neck, cutting the poor man's hands to ribbons as he tried to fight him off. The crime may have amounted to a murder if one of Judson's ribs had not protected his heart from the knife. After Judson finally fell to the floor, unconscious, Williams made his way home – followed closely by Mason, who called him a coward for attacking his friend so viciously and for using a knife to settle an argument. In response, Williams turned to Mason and stabbed him in the stomach.

12 NOVEMBER 1887 This night George Bouckley, an elderly and seemingly pleasant inhabitant of Ironbridge, went to bed with his wife as

usual. By all reports, the two were a happily married couple who hardly ever argued. Nothing seemed out of the ordinary until Bouckley woke up in the early hours, picked up a pick axe, and struck out at his wife. During the murderous assault Bouckley fractured her skull and broke one of her arms. In the chaos that followed, Bouckley chased his wife out onto the street, and as she fled from him he threw his pick axe after her. It struck her on the head. Minutes later, Bouckley committed suicide by cutting his own throat. Why he suddenly snapped will never be known.

13 NOVEMBER 1838 On his way home, a young man by the name of Maddox was travelling through Old Park when a fatal accident took place. Although the exact details of how the accident occurred are unknown, what is known is that the man was found, drowned, underneath his cart at the bottom of the canal on this day. The horse was still attached to the cart. The scene was discovered by a young boy who was passing by and noticed the wheels of the cart protruding from the canal.

14 NOVEMBER 1501 On this day Arthur, the Prince of Wales, married Catherine of Aragon at St Paul's Cathedral before travelling to their new home, Ludlow Castle. The couple did not have much of a chance to settle down and enjoy married life at the castle, as Prince Arthur became quickly and dangerously ill, dying a few short months after their arrival,

Catherine of Aragon, bottom, the first of Henry VIII's wives, married Prince Arthur on this day. (Wikimedia Commons)

on the 2 April, at the young age of 15. The exact cause of Prince Arthur's death is unknown, but some historians argue that it may have been consumption, diabetes or the 'sweating sickness', which some believe to have been hantavirus (a life-threatening disease similar to the flu, which is spread by rodents). Although Catherine also became sick, she was able to recover. After the death of her late husband, it was arranged that the young widow would marry Arthur's brother, Henry, in an attempt to preserve good relations with Spain. As history has shown, her better-known second wedding was not destined to be much happier than her first.

15 NOVEMBER 1635 Thomas 'Old Tom' Parr was a Shropshire native who lived for 152 years – or so the legend goes. Parr was born near Shrewsbury in 1483, in a time when the national average life expectancy was 32 years. He supposedly joined the army in the year 1500. The bachelor did not marry until his eightieth year, but at this grand age he bore two children. To make the story even more surreal, Old Tom Parr was meant to have had an affair at the age of 100 and fathered another child through his mistress before remarrying at 122. He claimed that the reason for his good health and long years was his diet, which he said consisted of 'sub-rancid cheese and milk in every form, coarse and hard bread and small drink, generally sour whey'. He eventually moved down to London and was regarded as a spectacle, but it is said that this move prompted a sudden change in diet which ultimately contributed to his death. A post mortem apparently found that his internal organs were in a perfect state, and no real cause of death could be determined. He was buried in Westminster Abbey on this day. Recently, it has been determined that Parr may have been confused with his grandfather of the same name, which would explain his seeming longevity.

16 NOVEMBER 1932 On this day in Ironbridge, labourer Edward Bullock Parry (34) of Broseley was charged with the wilful murder of William John Page Phillips (22). The murder was committed on the 15th and the victim suffered for nearly a day before dying, also on this day, in the Lady Forester Hospital, Broseley.

17 NOVEMBER 1939 Wilfred George Howells (22), a bricklayer, was found guilty of the manslaughter of William Leslie Evans during the Shropshire Assizes. The incident occurred following a motor accident on this date. There was some speculation over whether Howells had been under the influence of alcohol, but he was found innocent of this accusation. The incident occurred due to the fact that Howells was driving too fast on the Ruyton road. At the trial the judge, a Mr Justice Hawke, said 'I am not one who likes severity for its own sake, and I am glad the jury have made a recommendation for leniency which enables me to strain it as far as I can'. He went on to sentence Howells to an extremely merciful six months in prison, as well as disqualifying him from driving for five years.

18 NOVEMBER 1922 At Emstrey Banks, Police Constable Brunt saw two teenagers trying to break into a house. When Brunt intervened, one of the young men reacted by aiming his revolver at the police officer. The shot fired, but thankfully luck was on Brunt's side and the bullet struck a brass numeral on his tunic, which saved him from injury and probable death. The two men, who were later identified as Cyril Gears and Percy Hickman, were arrested in Dawley later on in the day, and charged with attempted murder. Hickman was discharged as he had not been in possession of the weapon. Although Gears insisted that his intention had simply been to scare the officer, not to shoot him, he was committed for trial.

19 NOVEMBER 1796 Tom Moody of Willey Hall had an intense and on-going fear of one day being buried alive. This fear, which would be considered relatively irrational in this day and age, is known as taphophobia, and can be translated as 'fear of graves'. As irrational as it might seem now, back in the eighteenth century and before the birth of modern medicine, it was quite a common and justified fear. Throughout history, there have been countless examples of people being buried before their time and there have even been cases where individuals have woken up while being embalmed. Such accounts have been compiled by William Tebb, who accounted for 149 live burials, 219 near-live burials and ten cases of live dissections. In fact,

President George Washington was also known to have suffered from this fear, and demanded that he not be buried for two days after he had passed on. Moody was so obsessed that one day he might be locked in a coffin that, when he sensed that his life was coming to a close, he approached his master, Lord Forester, and begged of him a request. The request was as follows:

> When I am dead, I wish to be buried at Barrow under the yew trees, in the churchyard there. And to be carried to the grave by six earth stoppers and my old horse, with my whip, boots, spurs and cap slung on each side of the saddle. And the brush of the last fox when I was up at the death at the side of the forelock, and two couples of old hounds to follow me to the grave as mourners. When I am laid in the grave, let three halloos be given over to me and then, if I don't lift my head, you may fairly conclude that Tom Moody is dead.

Lord Forester was gracious enough to ensure that this request was followed. Moody was buried on this day, and thanks to his last request everyone was entirely positive that his biggest fear had not been realised.

20 NOVEMBER 1880 Local media reported on a fire that had broken out at Shrewsbury Guildhall, which might have been caused by the plumbers who had been working there days earlier. Despite the severe fire, and the fact that the roof and floor were totally destroyed, all of the valuable paintings were saved and there were no fatalities.

21 NOVEMBER 1838 *The Times* reported two sad deaths that occurred in the canal near Old Park on the 14th of this month. A man and wife were found drowned in the canal, and it appears that witnesses had seen the two arguing hours before they were found. The woman had left her house in order to visit a neighbour. The husband followed, and the lady, obviously infuriated, said that if he continued following her she would jump into the canal. He obviously did not foresee that she would go through with her plan, but when she leapt from the canal he jumped in right after her.

22 NOVEMBER 1774 Major-General Robert Clive, who is known better as Clive of India, was born in Styche, Market Drayton. During his childhood in Shropshire, he is said to have climbed Market Drayton's St Mary's Church and frightened passers-by from his position on one of the gargoyles. The troublesome boy was also expelled from three different schools, including Market Drayton Grammar School, but ultimately went on to have an extremely successful career. During his lifetime, Clive secured India for the Crown and was described by William Pit as the most eloquent person that he had ever met. Clive tried to kill himself a number of times, due to a long history of depression. He also suffered from gallstones, which caused him incredible pain. To numb the pain he used opium, causing him to develop an unfortunate addiction. Clive's final suicide attempt succeeded on this day after he stabbed himself with a penknife. Shropshire remains proud of the general, and honours him with a prominent statue in Shrewsbury Town Square.

23 NOVEMBER 1846 James Smith and Sarah Hill worked in the same factory in Bridgnorth. Hill had been carrying a torch for Smith for quite a while, but her feelings were never reciprocated. On 19 November, it appears that Hill went too far and said or did something to rile the man. Smith snapped and chased Hill around the workshop until at last he caught up with her and struck her hard in the stomach. This attack caused substantial internal injuries through the rupturing of her intestines. She was taken home immediately, but sadly died from her injuries on this day after four days of agony.

24 NOVEMBER 1953 Following a failed appeal on the 12 January, a gardener by the name of Desmond Donald Hooper (27) was executed on 26 January 1954. The crime he committed was the murder of Elizabeth 'Betty' Selina Smith (12). Her body had been found at the bottom of a 44ft air shaft, situated near an abandoned portion of the Shropshire Union Canal, on the 24 July. At the time, she had been missing for two days. During the trial Mr

William Lewis, for the prosecution, revealed that the child had been fully clothed but had serious injuries all over her body and a man's tie around her throat. The autopsy showed that she had been partially strangled before being thrown down the shaft, but that she would still have been alive when she fell. A solid motive was never really established, although there is some reason to believe that the violent act may have come about after Hooper discovered that Smith had hit one of his sisters. Following the trial on 24 November 1953, Hooper was sentenced to death.

25 NOVEMBER 1887 Elijah Bowers Forrester of Whixall was brought before the magistrates at Whitchurch on this date. Forrester was alleged to have shot his brother-in-law, William Powell. The locals were both intrigued and incredibly unnerved, as this was the third reported murder in a week. On the fateful night, Powell's family heard two gun shots and the Powell's son went to investigate. Not far from his house he found his father lying dead on the road, a gunshot wound in his abdomen. Powell ultimately received fifteen years' penal servitude. Despite the fact that the two men were neighbours and family, they had a long-standing rivalry, which prompted Forrester to compose the following song:

> There was a man, an Indian red,
> Which all the neighbours do him dread,
> The cocks and hens begin to squeak,
> When into the hen roost he does sneak.
> The wind blew well, the bushes were dry,
> Says he, my fortune I mean to try;
> To rob the insurance was his intent,
> So he struck a match, and off it went;
> And when money he doth lack,
> Something has to go to rack;
> And to satisfy his foul desire,
> He set his own bedding on fire.

26   NOVEMBER 1887   On this day *The Times* reported that, at Otley, on the 25th, William Taylor was charged with the wilful murders of both his infant daughter, Annie, and of the superintendent of police, Mr Birkhill. At his inquest his wife, Hannah, was the chief witness and explained the circumstances of the shooting. Hannah claimed that Taylor had been suffering from fits on the days prior to the shooting, and had looked more and more disturbed. Hannah was growing increasingly frightened of her husband and had occasionally run out of the house for fear that he might try to kill her. Before the first shooting, Taylor was apparently calm, quietly smoking and staring into the fire. At some point, however, he snapped and killed both his daughter and Birkhill, who had come to arrest him, with a gun. Dr Bennett, a witness for the prosecution, claimed that little Annie's wound was approximately 5in by 4in, and that her lower spine had been completely shattered. Taylor was found guilty of two counts of wilful murder and immediately transported to Hollbeck station.

27   NOVEMBER 1649   On this day presentations were made at Court Leet in Ludlow regarding accusations about Margaret Bridgens. Bridgens had been accused of 'exorcising witchcrafts, charmings, sorceries, etc'. She fervently denied having any knowledge of witchcraft, or knowing anyone else who practiced witchcraft. The result of the trial and her fate is unknown. It was around this time, shortly after the end of the First English Civil War, that witch hunts became a problem in England. The general fear of witches grew into mass hysteria, and the period was later to be known as the 'Burning Times' around Europe. Of course, a woman burning at the stake is a familiar image from history, one often associated with the punishment of a witch. However, although this method of execution was common around mainland Europe, in England – as in North America – hanging was the preferred method. These witch hunts became prevalent as a sort of social rite of cleansing. As a society, people wanted a physical entity to blame for all of their misfortunes. It would have been around this time that, according to certain sources, Gideon Planke was in South

Shropshire. Planke was an infamous witch hunter who was working under a parliamentary mandate in Shropshire to find and bring to light witchcraft.

28 NOVEMBER 1913 On this day, local media reported on yet another mining accident. This one involved an 'assistant runner-on' by the name of Robert Churn (18), who worked for the Lilleshall Co. The incident had occurred the day before and it had, in fact, been Churn's first day working underground. He was given his orders by his boss, which included watching the main runner-on bringing the full tubs, one at a time, to the cage. He was instructed to observe carefully, as he would eventually be doing the same work. Everything went according to plan for the first hour of Churn's shift. He obviously felt confident that he had mastered the necessary skills, as the young man then asked the main runner-on if he could do some of the work by himself. Satisfied that Churn could handle the labour, the man consented but warned him to be vigilant and to keep his head low. The timbering was due to be raised by another shift of men at another point. Churn commenced work, moving in front of the tub to shift it. He grabbed the tub and was moving backward with it in his hands when he forgot to keep his head lowered. He had backed himself into a low bar and, as he wasn't immediately aware of this, he kept walking backward, meaning that his head became squashed between the tub and the bar. Acting on instinct, Churn dropped the tub and, in shock, fell down hard and landed on his back. He damaged his spinal cord and neck, injuries which worsened and eventually proved fatal on 6 January 1914.

29 NOVEMBER 1882 A somewhat drunk shaftsman by the name of Lewis Evans (25) was working in Minsterley on this day when he fell head first into a shaft. He was on the surface at the time, helping secure the ladder, so it would have been quite a fall. This seems to be one of those unlucky days for the miners of Shropshire, though given the number of mining accidents that have occurred in the county this may be unsurprising. For example, in 1865 Cotton (35), a collier, was working in Ironbridge with the Madeley Wood Colliery when a fall of coal today brought his life to a premature end.

In 1867, a miner called Evans (43) was working in Wellington with the Old Park Colliery when he, too, fell down a shaft to his death.

30 NOVEMBER 1867 Travelling salesman Barnatt Zusman was found dead on this day by a hunter's dog. Following an inquest it was revealed that he had last been seen alive on 15 November by a client named Aaron Gothmeir, who had given him valuables to sell. As he had gone missing – and more importantly, had not been sending Gothmeir the nightly reports as arranged – it was assumed that Zusman had gone on the run with the jewellery, and a warrant was put out for his arrest. It was rescinded when his corpse was discovered. Although a man named George Harris was tried for the crime, he was found not guilty. There was insufficient evidence to make another arrest, so no one was brought to justice for this crime.

DECEMBER

A war memorial in the Quarry, Shrewsbury depicts
St Michael and honours the men and women of
Shropshire who gave their lives for their country
in the First and Second World Wars.
(Photo by Samantha Lyon)

Morgan Jones of Diddlebury, who was charged with assaulting William Balk, was a member of the Ludlow Board of Guardians. (Photo by Samantha Lyon)

1 **DECEMBER** 1908 The *Shrewsbury Chronicle* reported on this day that, at Ludlow, Morgan Jones of Diddlebury, Craven Arms, was charged with assaulting William Balk (14), an orphan from the workhouse. The case was all the more shocking as the farmer had been a member of the Ludlow Board of Guardians.

2 **DECEMBER** 1079 On this day, knights rode into the castle of Mabel de Bellême, Countess of Shrewsbury, and cut off her head. Geoffrey White in *Transactions of the Royal Historical Society* describes her thus: she was 'small, very talkative, ready enough to do evil, shrewd and jocular, extremely cruel and daring.' Mabel had an incredible history, accidentally poisoning her own brother-in-law in an attempt to get at a family rival; her father had upped the stakes in the feud when he kidnapped the rival's father and mutilated him – at a wedding, of all places. The knights in question were angered by her (successful) attempts to steal their lands. They escaped the scene by destroying the bridge over which they fled, but were pursued by assassins sent by Mabel's children for years afterwards.

Police Constable Water wrongly imprisoned two Bavarian girls in order to get to Shrewsbury to see the races. (Library of Congress, LC-DIG-ppmsc-08835)

3   DECEMBER 1833 On this day, *The Times* reported the rather bizarre story that Police Constable Walter from Wenlock had imprisoned two Bavarian girls despite being entirely without appropriate warrants of committal. When he made the arrests and took the girls to Shrewsbury Gaol, they were not given any indication as to what they had done wrong or as to how long they would be remanded. When this was discovered, Walter was questioned. It turned out that he had made the arrest as a ruse to get to Shrewsbury, at the public's expense, to see the races.

4   DECEMBER 1910 Seven miners that were being carried in a cage to the bottom of a pit in the Kemberton Colliery crashed a distance of 388ft to the floor. Two of the miners, Randolph Cecil Miles and Albert Jones, were only 14 years of age. The other victims were Thomas Gelnister, George Gough Senior, Richard Rogers, Alphonso Stanley and Arthur Wilton. The *Shrewsbury News* would later describe the occurrence as, 'A shocking spectacle, the bodies being so mangled as to be almost beyond recognition.' Following their deaths, an inquest was held and it was revealed that the steel

rope that was used to lower the men had broken. A verdict of accidental death was returned following a trial, but the jury suggested that the colliery should 'adopt some device for safeguarding the persons who had to travel up and down the shaft.'

5 DECEMBER 1849 An inquest was held in Shrewsbury upon the death of a poor Welsh girl by the name of Jones. Jones resided at Craven Arms, and it seemed that the death occurred after a necessary operation that was undertaken to remove her eyeball. She gave her consent for the operation, but as a drug was being administered by the surgeon, Mr W.J. Clemont, a complication arose. Despite the fact that he had only so far given her one-third of the recommended dose, Jones began to seize with apoplexy, speaking feverishly in Welsh. Before Clemont could respond, the seizures came to an abrupt end and Jones passed away. The surgeon said that it was a reaction he had not seen before – and that she reacted as if she had just swallowed acid.

6 DECEMBER 1872 At this time mining and agriculture were the major industries in the country, with the mining of coal and ironstone being extremely important for the Industrial Revolution. This day saw the tragic Springwell Pit Disaster at Little Dawley, where eight young men (all under 22 years of age) fell to their deaths. After a hard day's work at the pit, the men attached themselves to the triple-linked chain and began the ascent to the surface. They were close to the top of the deep pit when the links snapped, causing the men to fall. They were then crushed by the heavy iron chain, hundreds of yards in length, which fell upon them. All but one of the men died instantly, and the remaining man died shortly after being brought up to the surface. The funeral at the Holy Trinity Church was attended by thousands of people, and the miners were all interred in one grave.

7 DECEMBER 1886 A violent gale began on this day and affected most of the country. In Shropshire, the gale caused the Severn to rise to

a dangerous level, and an old man named Laurence fell into the Severn and drowned.

8   DECEMBER   1691   Richard Baxter of Rowton (76) was a prominent and well-respected Church leader at this time. He eventually became a Nonconformist as a dissenting Puritan and proved to be a focal point for controversy. He developed an interest in Nonconformity to the Church of England during his time in Bridgnorth, where he found he disagreed with the Church on a number of matters. Baxter went on to write *Aphorisms of Justification*, which caused a lot of outrage upon its publication. In 1685 Baxter was brought before the infamous judge Sir George Jeffreys, also known as the hanging judge, and spent eighteen months in prison for libel. He kept preaching all the while, though, and is known to have said, 'I preached as one never sure to preach again and as a dying man to dying men.' In addition to this time in prison, he was also given a fine, and ordered to stay in prison until the fine was paid off. However, due to his old age he was released early and his fine was remitted by the government, who were hoping to win him over. He died on this day.

9   DECEMBER   1891   A destructive storm passed through the county, causing houses to be unroofed, chimneys to be demolished and structures to be blown away. When night came Mr and Mrs Hotchkiss, who ran the Horse Shoe Hotel in Dorrington, went to bed with their 3-year-old child. Three hours later the occupants of the hotel were woken by a loud crash, later determined to have been caused by the collapse of the chimney that ran up the side of the roof. The chimney had fallen through the wall and onto the Hotchkisses' bed, killing Mr Hotchkiss and seriously injuring his wife. The child miraculously escaped without injury.

10   DECEMBER   1944   John Henry Cound Brunt, a priest born at Priest Weston, died in Italy on this day. It was only four days before his 22nd birthday. During his short life, Brunt reached the rank of captain, became a recipient of the Victoria Cross and Military Cross, and was well known for

his considerate and kind nature. On this day he was sitting on a porch with some friends, enjoying a cup of tea, when a German mortar bomb landed right by his feet. When it went off, the explosion killed him instantly.

11 DECEMBER 1959 After a girl had been killed during a serious motorcycle accident, Malcolm John Mason (19), an airman of RAF Bridgnorth, leapt at the opportunity to steal a £20 watch from her wrist. He intended the watch to be given as a present to his fiancée. The watch had a modern-day value of around £381. Mason pled guilty to the crime and was fined £10.

12 DECEMBER 1840 Mrs Beddoes lived with some family in a farm house in Miston. The property had been left to her by her late husband, who had died fourteen years before. One night, at about 10 p.m., the household was jolted awake by the sound of a dog barking nearby. They all went to the window to see what was causing the ruckus, and saw – to their horror – that a number of men were lurking in the shadows around her house. Before they could act, one of the men broke open the door and dashed into their home. Beddoes had two sons, both of whom made their way downstairs to deal with the criminals. Unfortunately, the sons were overpowered, cowed by the dog, and the two ruffians made their way to the Beddoes' cellar where they stole a jug containing ninety sovereigns and five old guineas. They made their escape before the police could be notified, but were thankfully captured on this day.

13 DECEMBER 1955 Parts of England suffered extreme temperatures at this time, and experienced substantial snowfalls. Ten glider pilots who had been trapped for three days in their club headquarters at Long Mynd due to the snow managed to escape on this day and walk to the village of Asterton.

Ten glider pilots were trapped for three days in their club headquarters at the Long Mynd in 1955 due to the snow. (Photo by Samantha Lyon)

14 DECEMBER 1855 On this night at Oswestry, a rather grumpy-looking old man was travelling through town with his wife and six children, desperately looking for a place to sleep. He knocked on the door of Shrewsbury Prison, and complained of being poor, hungry, and unable to find a place to shelter his family for the night. The jailer, Mr Williams, was sympathetic, as it was extremely cold outside. He therefore said that he and his family could stay in a cell for one night, but they would have to make other arrangements in the morning. As the beggar began to make himself at home, Williams thought that it might be wise to search the man in case the whole incident proved to be a ruse. The search revealed that the man, whose name turned out to be Patrick Middle, was far from poor: in fact, Williams produced several sovereigns and a silver and gold watch from the man's coat. It was eventually discovered that these treasures had been stolen by Middle, from various locations, as he made his way around the country.

15 DECEMBER 1935 Air Pilot Dorothy Clive of Market Drayton decided to take her cousin, Roger David Clive, for a flight on this day. Unfortunately, the snowstorm that they flew into caused Dorothy to hit a tree near Stoke-on-Trent Aerodrome. She suffered cuts and slight injuries, but her cousin was not so lucky and had to be admitted to Longton Hospital to recover from his severe head and leg injuries.

16 DECEMBER 1939 On this day there were two coincident sound tests in Shropshire and other Midland counties, all at 12.30 p.m., of the air-raid warning sirens erected for civil defence. When members of the public heard these civil-defence sirens, they were meant to stop what they were doing and head for shelter.

17 DECEMBER 1857 On this day *The Times* reported on the death of George Norton, a gamekeeper for Richard Corbet of Adderley Park, who had been involved in a fight. It seems that sixteen of the keepers were engaged in conflict with approximately forty poachers, during which Norton received severe injuries. These injuries were too serious for him to

hold any real chance of recovery, and he died not long after. Four men were tried for the crime and all served sentences for manslaughter. Twenty years later, on 12 March 1877, *The Times* followed this story up by reporting that William Taylor had been indicted on a charge of murder. He had been at a pub in Eccleshall on the 31 December when, in front of many witnesses, he admitted to being present at the fight. He claimed to have killed Norton by stabbing him through with a spear. This was eventually brought to trial, where Taylor pleaded not guilty. Four witnesses from the incident twenty years ago were brought forward for questioning. Three of the witnesses said that they had no idea who he was, and the forth said that, although he looked familiar, he was unable to identify him accurately. As the case hence hinged completely on Taylor's confession, it had to be dropped due to insufficient evidence.

18 DECEMBER 1896 The county suffered what the *Hawera & Normanby Star* would later refer to as a 'severe earthquake'. In parts of the county, including Darley, the quake lasted a minute and a half, and was preceded by a noise like a hurricane.

19 DECEMBER 1917 In the summer of the previous year Thomas Cox (59) was tried for the murder of his wife, Elizabeth. The two were at their Ludlow home when Cox produced a razor following an argument and slit her throat. He then cut his own throat after he realised the enormity of what he had done. The two were discovered by their son on 11 August: the boy walked in to his parents' bedroom and saw them lying in bed, covered in blood, with slits across both of their necks. The son inspected his parents, and realised his mother was dead. However, he immediately found medical assistance for his father, who recovered. Cox was sentenced to death and, following an unsuccessful appeal, was hanged on this day.

20 DECEMBER 1841 Mary Harries lived with her husband, Thomas Harries, in a cottage at Whixall, approximately 3 miles from Wem. Thomas had two children from a previous marriage, with his first wife having died

years before. The couple shared the cottage with Mary's parents, who tended to complain about their parenting style and give constant, unwanted advice. Over time this must have pushed the couple over the edge as, on this day, Mary Harries and her husband put into action a sinister plan involving poisoned flour. Mary cooked up a batch of apple dumplings for dinner. Eliza Williams, Mary's mother, ate part of a dumpling and was instantly sick. She suffered unbearable stomach pains and never recovered. By 9 p.m. that night she was dead. Mary's father, Arthur Williams, thankfully refused to eat the dumpling as he was already feeling extremely ill. It later surfaced that he'd had just enough of the food to make himself sick to the stomach, but not enough to endanger his life. In a desperate attempt to rid the house of evidence, Mary gave the remainder of the dumplings to the neighbours, which were consumed by their unfortunate son.

21 DECEMBER 1938 Local media reported on the death of acting pilot officer W.A. Jenns (20). Jenns attended the Flying Training School at Ternhill, and died in the Royal Salop Infirmary on the 20th from injuries he had suffered during a flying accident near Market Drayton.

22 DECEMBER 1868 Following the South Shropshire election riots, thirteen people at Church Stretton were brought before a full bench of magistrates. The charges that were read out included counts of criminal damage, concerning the breaking of the windows at the Church Stretton Hotel, doing damage to the extent of £35.

23 DECEMBER 1647 The Dingle, an enclosed garden within the Quarry, is said by many to be haunted by the ghost of a Mrs Foxall. She was burnt at the stake on this day for the crime of witchcraft and for killing her husband with a dose of poison.

24 DECEMBER 1848 At the Three Crowns pub in Wellington, George Taylor and Thomas Morrall were enjoying a drink when they noticed a number of Irishmen in the pub. When the Irishmen begun to sing, Taylor became increasingly annoyed and told them to keep it down. Then, to further illustrate his annoyance, he produced a pocket knife from below the table and placed it rather deliberately in front of him. After being asked what he was going to do with it, Taylor replied that the knife will 'do mischief' and that he was going to 'put it into some of the Irishmen'. He was kicked out of the pub by the landlord and was followed shortly by Morrall. One of the Irishmen, Francis Cunningham, was quietly walking home and was stopped by Taylor, who punched him in the stomach, winding him. He then produced the knife and stabbed him in the stomach. Cunningham did not die immediately, but lived through a few days of agony before finally passing away. Taylor was indicted for wilful murder, and sentenced to transportation for life.

25 DECEMBER 1841 On this day a servant, who worked for the respected farmer Mr Leighton, was visiting Shrewsbury to enjoy Christmas. This oblivious servant was soon coaxed aboard a boat that was moored in the canal. On-board were William Oakes, the captain, and David Jones, a boatman. The men offered the servant a drink containing an unknown but painful drug, which instantly knocked him out.

He was then robbed of his money and shoes and pushed overboard, still unconscious. The men, by now armed, fought off a number of others who had overheard the ruckus and come to investigate, before seriously injuring and robbing one of the party. Happily these criminals were eventually captured by a policeman and a watchman before being brought before Mr Badger, the mayor.

26 DECEMBER 1878 On the evening of the 12th Thomas Davies returned home, drunk and in an extremely bad mood. No one can ever know exactly what happened that night but, when the case came to court, witnesses claimed to have heard his wife cry, 'Don't, Thomas!' His young daughter then ran downstairs to find her mother lying unconscious on the floor. The victim was taken upstairs and looked after by Davies and his daughter, but no one called for a doctor until the 16th. Unfortunately there was no real chance of recovery by this time and Mrs Davies died on this day. A post mortem was conducted, and the doctor reached the conclusion that the death was due to an effusion of blood on the brain, which was most likely caused by an external injury to the back of the head. Things were looking bleak for Davies during his trial at Shrewsbury until his son testified and told the court that his father wasn't to blame. His mother, he claimed, had suffered a fit at the time and fallen over, which must have caused the injury. As there was no way to rule this out, Davies was found not guilty of manslaughter and released.

27 DECEMBER 1878 This year saw the occurrence of an excessive and disruptive winter. The average temperature across most of the Midlands and Southern England was below 0°C, a severe stretch that lasted until the end of January 1879. As a country, we have never dealt expertly with such extremes and at the time the boatmen of the Shropshire Union Canal were becoming increasingly annoyed. This day marked the third week that the Shropshire Union Canal was blocked up with ice, and as the boatmen only got paid when the canal was moving their incomes were severely impeded.

28 DECEMBER 1925 Following a tragic motor accident at Craven Arms on this day, four people lost their lives. An inquest began on the 30th, but it was put on hold for a fortnight after the identities of the victims were discovered. Among the deceased were Samuel Northway of Cardiff, a fish and fruit merchant, and his wife. A blind, retired farmer from Wentnor by the name of Pinches was also killed, along with William John Francis, the young child of a hotel employee from Church Stretton; his mother was also injured in the crash, but made a complete recovery.

29 DECEMBER 1927 An inquest was held on the body of a gypsy violinist by the name of Isaiah Lock (65). Lock had been found dead on the northern slopes of Long Mountain, buried in the snow. The coroner attested that his tragic death was due to a heart attack that was brought on by exposure to the extreme weather.

30 DECEMBER 1868 On this day *The Times* reported a tragic accident that occurred at Shrewsbury railway station on the 28th. A passenger by the name of Smith, who was accompanying his sister and mother to Leaton, was killed while waiting on the platform for the train to pull up. Smith was seen standing very close to the edge and, just as he was being waved back from the side of the platform, he fell and disappeared beneath the train. Eight carriages, all heavily freighted, passed over him and when he was finally retrieved he was alive but horribly mutilated. He died being carried to the Royal Salop Infirmary.

31 DECEMBER 1916 Sergeant Herbert Stokes served as part of the 3rd Shropshire Light infantry and was sent home from the front to recover from a wound. However, he was found dead at Pembroke Dock, with a rifle close by, after an apparent suicide.

BIBLIOGRAPHY

BOOKS

Glover, George, *Shropshire Murders* (Stoke-on-Trent: Arch, 1992)
Harrison, Paul, *Murder Casebook* (Berkshire: Countryside Books, 1994)
Sly, Nicola, *Shropshire Murders* (Stroud: The History Press, 2009)
Wood, Martin, *Shrewsbury Crime and Punishment* (Stroud: The History Press, 2008)

JOURNALS & NEWSPAPERS

Edinburgh Medical and Surgical Journal, Volume 22 (1824)
The Shropshire Star
The Times

Lightning Source UK Ltd.
Milton Keynes UK
UKOW04f1254231013

219630UK00003B/3/P